BIOMETRIC EMBEDDED SYSTEMS WITH ARDUINO

Unlocking the Power of Embedded C for Fingerprint Recognition and Access Control

By

Mikasa Mizuki

TABLE OF CONTENTS

INTRODUCTION ENGLISH 6

GETTING TO KNOW ABOUT THE FLAME SENSOR 8

FLAME SENSOR MODULE WAVELENGTH APPLICATION CONSIDERATION 9

HARDWARE REQUIREMENTS AND WIRING TO AN ARDUINO 11

CODE FIRE DETECTION USING ARDUINO AND FLAME SENSOR 12

GETTING TO KNOW ABOUT THE RAIN SENSOR MODULE 15

HARDWARE REQUIREMENTS AND WIRING TO AN ARDUINO 17

CODE RAIN SENSOR MODULE 19

REAL TIME DEMONSTRATION RAIN SENSOR MODULE 21

ARDUINO TO ARDUINO SERIAL COMMUNICATION 22

CIRCUIT CONNECTION OF TWO ARDUINOS 24

CODE ARDUINO RECEIVER DATA 25

CODE ARDUINO SENDING DATA 27

MODULE SPECIFICATION RF 433MHZ TRANSMITTER RECEIVER MODULE WITH ARDUINO 29

HARDWARE REQUIREMENTS AND WIRING TO AN ARDUINO 31

CODE RF 433MHZ RECEIVER MODULE TO AN ARDUINO 32

CODE RF 433MHZ TRANSMITTER MODULE TO AN ARDUINO 34

ARDUINO CAPACITIVE TOUCH SENSOR 36

CODING AND REAL 37

GETTING TO KNOW ABOUT THE BIO 39

WINDOWS SOFTWARE HARDWARE REQUIREMENTS AND WIRING TO AN ARDUINO 41

DOWNLOAD AND INSTALL THE WINDOWS SOFTWARE APPLICATION 42

ENROLLING FINGERPRINT USING WINDOWS SOFTWARE 46

TESTING THE ENROLLED FINGERPRINT USING ARDUINO IDE 48

ENROLLING AND SEARCHING FINGERPRINT USING ARDUINO IDE..50

INTRODUCTION TO ARDUINO MICROCONTROLLER 52

FEATURES OF ARDUINO MICROCONTROLLER 54

PIN LAYOUT & PORT STRUCTURE OF ARDUINO MICROCONTROLLER 56

HARDWARE & SOFTWARE USED IN THIS COURSE PART – 1...........59

HARDWARE & SOFTWARE USED IN THIS COURSE PART – 2...........61

DOWNLOADING ARDUINO IDE SOFTWARE 63

INTRODUCTION TO ARDUINO IDE...64

FEATURES OF ARDUINO IDE..66

EMBEDDED C REGISTER BIT MANIPULATION TECHNIQUES PART – 1 77

EMBEDDED C REGISTER BIT MANIPULATION TECHNIQUES PART – 2 89

INTERFACING LED WITH ARDUINO 96

7 SEGMENT DISPLAY WORKING EXPLAINED.....................................99

INTERFACING 7 SEGMENT DISPLAY WITH ARDUINO.................... 105

16X2 LIQUID CRYSTAL DISPLAY WORKING EXPLAINED................. 111

INTERFACING 16X2 LCD WITH ARDUINO....................................... 114

INPUT DEVICES WORKING LOGICS EXPLAINED............................. 123

INTERFACING PUSHBUTTON WITH ARDUINO 125

ELECTRO-MECHANICAL RELAY WORKING EXPLAINED.................. 130

INTERFACING RELAY WITH ARDUINO 140

INTERRUPTS IN MICROCONTROLLER EXPLAINED 144

IMPLEMENTING EXTERNAL INTERRUPT IN ARDUINO................... 149

TIMER INTERRUPT MODE FUNCTIONALITY EXPLAINED 158

IMPLEMENTING TIMER INTERRUPT PROGRAM IN ARDUINO MICROCONTROLLER... 161

TIMER OUTPUT COMPARE MODE FUNCTIONALITY EXPLAINED .. 165

REGISTER CONFIGURATION FOR TIMER OUTPUT COMPARE MODE IN ARDUINO MICROCONTROLLER.. 168

GENERATING PULSES USING TIMER OUTPUT COMPARE MODE IN ARDUINO MICROCONTROLLER 175

TIMER INPUT CAPTURE MODE FUNCTIONALITY EXPLAINED........ 178

MEASURING TIME DURATION OF PULSE USING TIMER INPUT CAPTURE MODE IN ARDUINO 181

PWM (PULSE WIDTH MODULATION) FUNCTIONALITY EXPLAINED 186

REGISTER CONFIGURATION FOR PWM SIGNAL GENERATION IN ARDUINO MICROCONTROLLER 191

GENERATING PULSES OF REQUIRED FREQUENCY AND DUTY CYCLE USING PWM IN ARDUINO 198

ANALOG TO DIGITAL CONVERTOR WORKING EXPLAINED 203

ADC REGISTER CONFIGURATION IN ARDUINO 211

LED DIMMER USING ADC AND PWM IN ARDUINO....................... 217

UART SERIAL COMMUNICATION WORKING EXPLAINED 223

REGISTER CONFIGURATION FOR ESTABLISHING UART IN ARDUINO MICROCONTROLLER... 226

HC-05 BLUETOOTH MODULE TESTING 236

INTERFACING HC-05 BLUETOOTH MODULE WITH ARDUINO....... 239

I2C INTER-INTEGRATED CIRCUITS COMMUNICATION WORKING EXPLAINED.. 243

REGISTER CONFIGURATION FOR ESTABLISHING I2C COMMUNICATION IN ARDUINO PART – 1................................... 252

REGISTER CONFIGURATION FOR ESTABLISHING I2C COMMUNICATION IN ARDUINO PART – 2................................... 258

INTERFACING 24CXX EEPROM WITH ARDUINO USING I2C COMMUNICATION 263

INTRODUCTION ENGLISH

Slow learners reading from me in this school have come up with that for sure you find different projects let see one by one. The first part of this section is jumping the fence and up in the second project. Since our ardiuno allows you to make sure that you wash away on a level when you detect whether it's raining or not. That is how you can get it done using you are awesome and also using for that with the up. Or if you're going to end the civil war what you are doing. You see, the project is quite different. We use the digital capacity that we know to light up the lamp with a single data. And the logic is based on biometric fingerprints and so on. It says use your logic that the biometrics all in one single or make anything up in detection and verification.

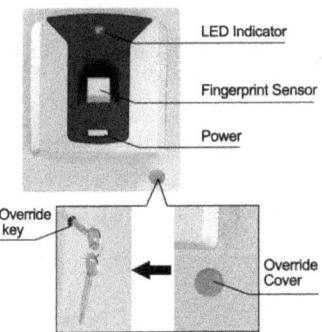

This model is used to say that it is a type of speech that does the rendering calculation feature finding and searching. I hope you go about building this body. I want to shut the board with you so that you get the project by yourself.

GETTING TO KNOW ABOUT THE FLAME SENSOR

Get to know about it. In this project they'll show you the flame sensor. This fits within our tree no to claim we have connected the LCD. I suppose we are trying to indicate the plane. We see the usage of the model.

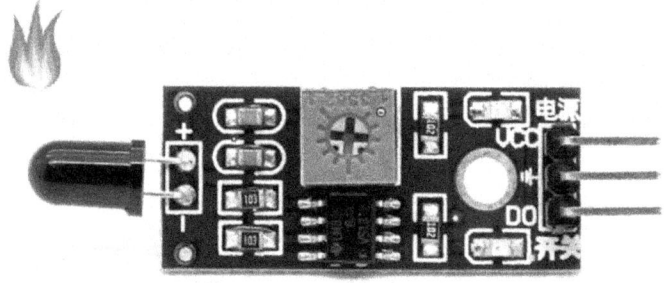

This type of sensor is used for some strange white detection and can be used to monitor projects or as a safety precaution to cut devices on and off. See the pin out connection for claims to send some more. Only three connections are required to allow this device to work with your Arduino. Here you can see the description of the flame sense of pins pin or component white quite DC supply input output goes low. When Plim is detected GNB clown input plane indicator and human needs. When Plim since sensitivity is just CW is more sensitive. CCW is less sensitive. Your detector has a 60 degree angle and is sensitive to the wavelength.

FLAME SENSOR MODULE WAVELENGTH APPLICATION CONSIDERATION

Literacy the application consideration of this module as previously mentioned the viewing angle is at 60 degrees. The sense that view is incredibly important as you design your project. How does it work? Claims into a model airplane that claims somebody will be x wavelength from 760 nanometer to eleven hundred nine meter.

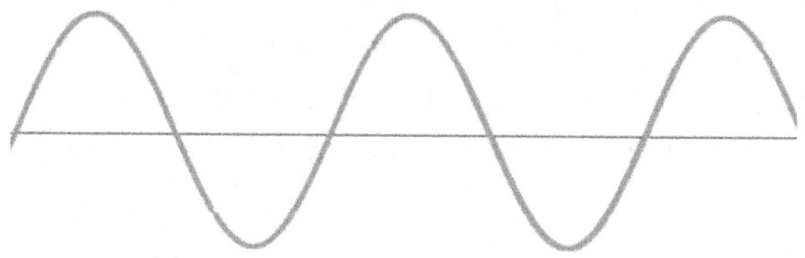

wavelengths from 760nm-1100nm

The other source of heat that will also detect this we've learned it is therefore important that you ensure that the only source of this particular range will be the flame that you want to detect. Otherwise your project may be riddled with Paul's measurements. Spot detection: Why is the device? I used a defective light. It took several attempts to see a plane. However each time I tried to spot from the light the GOSTA DO flash.

HARDWARE REQUIREMENTS AND WIRING TO AN ARDUINO

Start reading the project literacy list of hardware components required for this project Arduino you know flame sensor and the buzzer jumper wires like they are not the only source or who are into an Arduino. Now let us connect the Arduino to the plane sensor more to the wire sensor the Arduino.

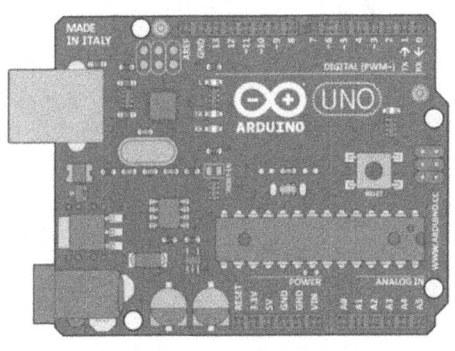

Simply connect the following as shown in the circuit diagram plym sensor interfacing to the Arduino plane sensor BCSC to Arduino five whole plane sensor ground to plan and the locking up flame sensor to Reno and alloc been easy to the realtime output voltage signals on the thermal resistance LCD interfacing to Arduino Elodie positive been connected to 90 percent of Arduino negative when the ground pin up Arduino was positive when connected to the world of Arduino negative spin to ground pin of Arduino.

CODE FIRE DETECTION USING ARDUINO AND FLAME SENSOR

Now we will see the complete code for this project. Tarty Arduino I'll use the following code maps and the analog values given by the flame sensor 0 2 1 0 2 4 the stop claim sensor will have the following reaction with this code. If holding a beam in front of the sensor al-Libi and Bowser will be activated and a fire detector will be sent to the Seagle monitor. If not, Plim is detected in front of the sensor LCD and Buzza will be deactivated and no fire will be sent to the CEL monitor. To view the output point of a single monitor at your Arduino this code is constantly updating to provide real time feedback of the flame sensor.

```
#include<SoftwareSerial.h>
int sensorPin = A0;
int sensorValue = 0;
int led = 9;
int buzzer = 12

void setup() {
pinMode(led, OUTPUT);
pinMode(buzzer,OUTPUT);
Serial.begin(9600);
}

void loop()
{
Serial.println("Welcome to Makerdemy");
sensorValue = analogRead(sensorPin);
Serial.println(sensorValue);

if (sensorValue < 20)
{
Serial.println("Fire Detected");
Serial.println("LED on");
digitalWrite(led,HIGH);
```

The program is pretty straightforward. It uses the Elodie connected to pin 9 of the serial monitor. Pure Arduino ID to see the output Sellick the input being for the LBA people who stored the value coming from the sensor output for the LCD output pin port was a big player. The

Ellaby pin and Buzza as an output here based on our condition that trace all value is less than 20 for the plane sensor. As you can see here if the sensor value is less than 20 we are printing for the day and the LCD goes high and if the condition is not me and the buzz will be low now come by and upload the code bit by operation of the plane detector module and just sensitivity open the monitor on your Arduino program move a plane in and out of the viewing angle of the same the result is displayed in the serial window.

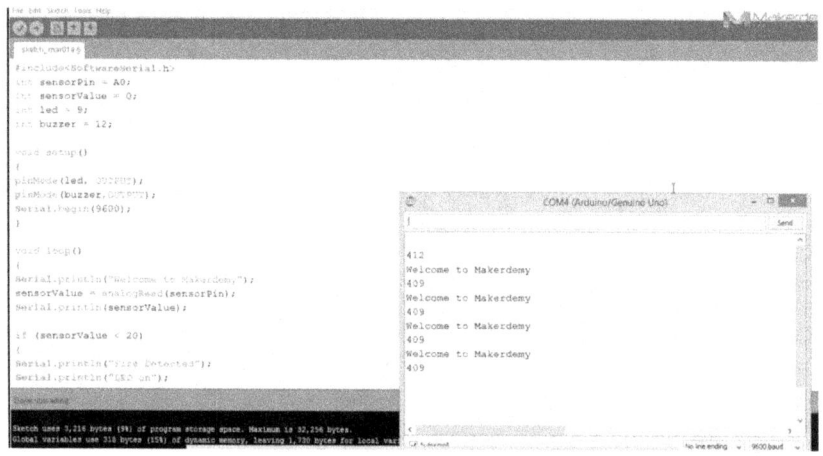

When it is clean the al-Libi is automatically done on and when diddies Norfleet are automatically done. All Ellaby and Buzza the Reaser are displayed in the Sebille window.

GETTING TO KNOW ABOUT THE RAIN SENSOR MODULE

Arduino then sends someone to Raincy somebody allows you to Mazer moisture via analog output pins and it provides a digital output when a trace of moisture level is exceeded their instance of margin is based on the L-M 390 or the ampere. It includes the electronics Mordieu on a printed circuit board that collects the raindrops as the raindrop is collected on the circuit board. They create part of Bar-Lev existence that are measured by the O.P. ampere. The Lord's Resistance or the more water the lower the voltage output Conversely the less water the greater the output voltage of the end alaap in a completely dry board for example will cost them more fuel to output 5 volts here.

THE LESS WATER

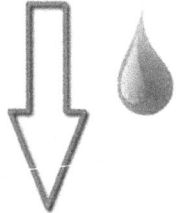

GREATER THE OUTPUT VOLTAGE
OF THE ANALOG PIN

Let's see a quick and simple start guide for using and exploring the real sense of more do with the adrenal getting to know about 13 cents or more usage when sensor used in the detection of water beyond what a humidity sensor can detect how it works. The range sensor detects water that completes the circuit; only the centerboard printed leaves the sensor board acting as a variable resistor that will change from 100 kilo ohms. When we do to make our homes and drive in shot the record doubled the more current that will be conducting. Let's see the pin up connection up there in a sense more when the sensor module pin out diagram for the location and description of various pins controls and indicators VCC positive fiberboard Basus GNT. Gone are negative power source digital output goes low when moisture exceeds set thresholds. Is zero analog output zero to five polls. The lower the voltage the greater the moisture power clearly indicates the power is applied. Output Ellerby illuminates when moisture has exceeded the threshold set by sensitivity adjustment. Sensitivity adjustment counter-clockwise is more sensitive Kantar anti-clockwise is less sensitive.

HARDWARE REQUIREMENTS AND WIRING TO AN ARDUINO

Start building the project. Let's see what hardware components are required to build this Arduino range instead of a more dual model with an analog output along the. Jump wise wiring to an adrenal. Now let us connect the you know the rain sensor model to either instance of the Arduino simply connect the following as shown in the circuit diagram hardware connection sensor interfacing to the Arduino sensor BCSE to Arduino fireball.

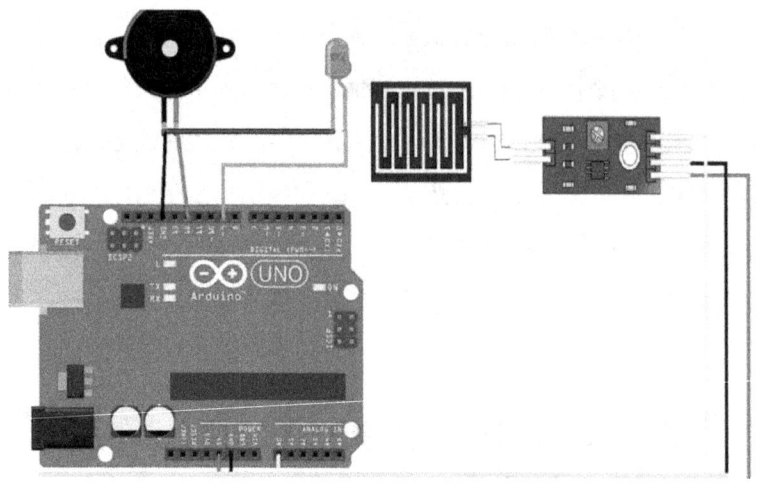

Gaon and alaap have been offering a sensor to Arduino analog. The realtime output voltage signals on the thermal resistance lupins range sensor to censor board positive to censor board. Hook up the negative censor board hook up the LCD in the PC to Arduino the positive be connected to 9 pin up Arduino make it been connected to ground pin up or bring no buzzer interfacing to a dream buzzer or been connected to the world of Arduino negative spin connected to ground in the Arduino.

CODE RAIN SENSOR MODULE

Now let us see the complete code for this project. Study ID. The following code maps and uses the analog values given by that sensor. That Gatti's between 0 2 1 0 2 3 it. The analog output provides a moisture level at 1 0 2 3 is high which means there is no printing if the analog value is less than 400.

```
Rainsensor
#include<SoftwareSerial.h>

int sensorPin = A0;
int sensorValue = 0;
int led = 9;
int buzzer = 12;

void setup() {
pinMode(led, OUTPUT);
pinMode(buzzer, OUTPUT);
Serial.begin(9600);
}

void loop()
{
Serial.println("Welcome to Makerdemy Rainwater Sensor");
sensorValue = analogRead(sensorPin);
Serial.println(sensorValue);
```

It prints a message in warning and if the value goes less than 200 It gives an alert message as you can see here the rain sensor pin is connected to and alaap being easy to the default sensor value is assigned as zero. We have defined the Elodie pin as nine and the buzzer pin as dual under the white set of Ponson we are declaring the Elodie and Bozer as output inside the white fonts then we are printing the message. Welcome to make or D-MI this message will be printed in the seal Monico. Here we are reading the analog value from the sensor pin and printing the seam in the CVN monitor. Now let us come to a condition. If the sensor value goes below 100 it will bring the message flood and it will enable the LCD and deposit.

```
Rainsensor
if (sensorValue < 200)
{
Serial.println("Flood");
digitalWrite(led, HIGH);
digitalWrite(buzzer, HIGH);
delay(1000);
}

else if (sensorValue < 400)
{
Serial.println("Rain Warning");
tone(12, 440, 200);
digitalWrite(led, HIGH);
delay(200);
noTone(8);
digitalWrite(led, LOW);
delay(300);
}
```

We have also mentioned our delay of a thousand milliseconds. Let us see if the condition of the sensor value falls below less than 400. The program will generate rewarming. We have a sign I speak to one for this buzzer by passing the mail you google for 440 and 200 this conviction blinks to Elodie for 200 milliseconds and then the Ellaby is turned up. Now let's see if none of the conditions are made. The program will come to a spot where it is Zoom's that there is no rainfall on the LCD and the Bozza will be up. Which is shown using the low signal now. Compile and upload the code into the Arduino board as you can see our compilation is successful. We have uploaded the code on the board.

REAL TIME DEMONSTRATION RAIN SENSOR MODULE

Running the program the sketch will begin immediately uploading. Open your cereal window and view the results for a little water as launch works well on board the sensor and see the level moisture decreases.

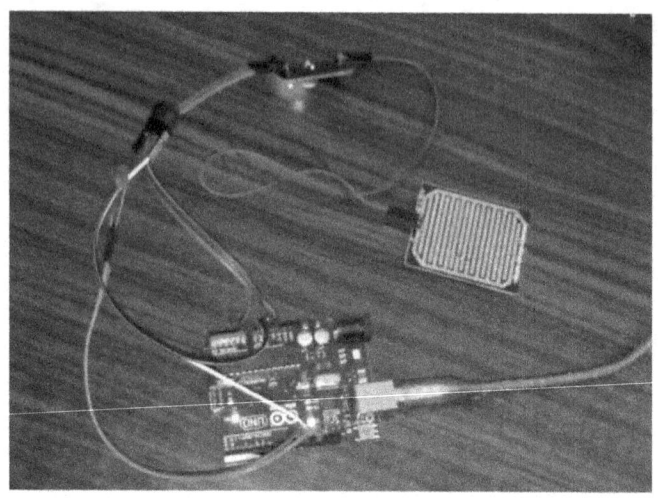

If you get the board work of the Syrian monitor should indicate that it is raining. If not, try turning the sensitivity adjustment clockwise or.

ARDUINO TO ARDUINO SERIAL COMMUNICATION

Arduino who are Arduino serial communication transmission between do adrenal, maybe sometimes we want to share the workload of our brain or with an adult, though maybe we want more digital or analog. An integrated circuit is the base solution. It is usually used to communicate between components on motherboards in cameras. Any embedded electronic system here will make an entire integrated circuit bus using adrenals. We will program one Mostert Arduino to command the other slave Arduino to blink. It's believed in Elodie once or twice depending on the receiver value.

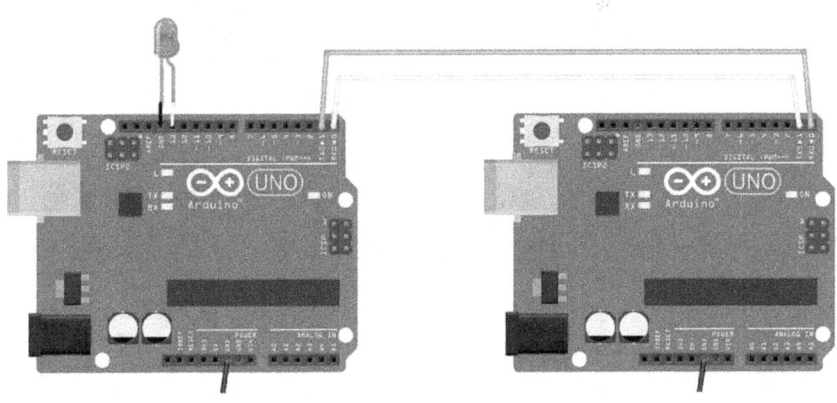

Let us start building the project. Let us see what hardware components are required for this project. Who are Renos and the jumper wires? It is possible for Gene adrenals to be that in such a way as to get communication between the two adrenals. Happy are they not too Arduino communication can be useful for many projects such as having one adrenal who run motors and having another sister surroundings and then really come on to the other

Arduino it can be done in several methods using the integrated circuit and serial this project focused on Arduino to Arduino communication through the serial ports are x and t x.

CIRCUIT CONNECTION OF TWO ARDUINOS

Wiring to an Arduino the circuit diagram shows how to connect the two or three notes together. But if there is no makeup,

It can be connected to any of the serial ports on the Amiga as long as they're accounted for in the code. There has to be a common ground between the two. Or else it will not function properly. Also note that the XP goes to Onyx and Alex goes to the X attach and L.E. the PIN number 13. The law only goes to pin 13 The shortly goes to ground.

CODE ARDUINO RECEIVER DATA

Now we will see the complete code for this project. First we will see the Arduino receiver data code for this project here. The Elodie is attached to pin number 13 in coming by. Is a very able to read incoming serial data under-sea it up Hunsdon we are initializing the serial communication with the Ballbreaker up 9600 the al-Libi pin has been declared as output under each condition if the serial value is more than zero it will read the oldest byte in the serial buffer.

```
const int ledPin = 13;
int incomingByte;

void setup() {
  Serial.begin(9600);
  pinMode(ledPin, OUTPUT);
}

void loop() {
  if (Serial.available() > 0) {
    incomingByte = Serial.read();
    if (incomingByte == 'H') {
      digitalWrite(ledPin, HIGH);
    }
    if (incomingByte == 'L') {
      digitalWrite(ledPin, LOW);
    }
  }
}
```

And once it is read it will be stored in-coming by variable. Now let us compare the incoming byte is equal to the character H if with the digital pin there will be anybody high on the LCD we'll go this. The other case if the incoming byte is an LCD will be done all. Now compile and upload this code into the Arduino the project code uses the Arduino board to receive data from the computer. In this case the Arduino board turns on an LCD when it receives the character edge and tons of the Elodie when it receives the character. That data can be sent from the Arduino ID CDL monitor or under that program.

CODE ARDUINO SENDING DATA

Now let us see the Arduino sending data code for this project. When sending things to CVN everything is sent in bytes. These bikes are then read one byte at a time by the other Arduino. When it is just characters sent to the Sebille it is relatively easy to convert from characters to bytes. However if there are both Kadek those numbers are going to this can lead to messing up the data because a number and the character can have the same value.

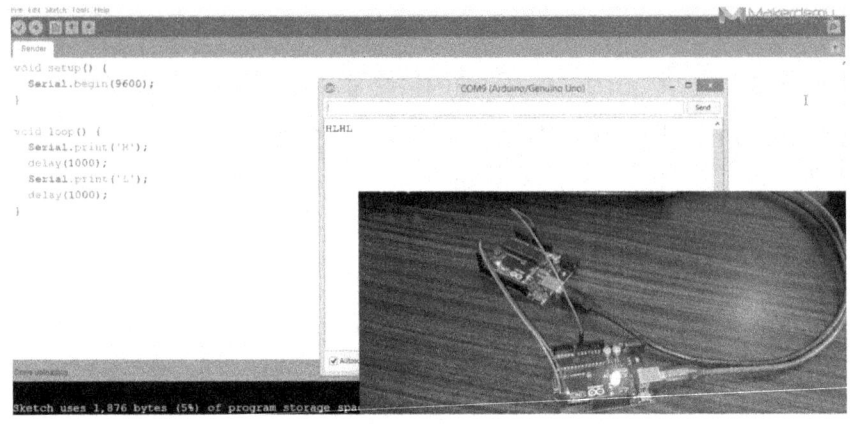

But that does not make them the same numbers are also tricky because they may not fit into the byte compiled and upload this code into the other Arduino when the program run the Elodie access to print voting on the Arduino with the Arduino receiver data are called flash on and off at the frequency of 0.5 foes to make sure that code doing that their beliefs can be changed in the ever code and this code. The job of edge was to turn Elahi on and the job of an was to turn the energy off. It can be easily applicable to behavior as characters trigger more reactions.

MODULE SPECIFICATION RF 433MHZ TRANSMITTER RECEIVER MODULE WITH ARDUINO

How to use 4:33 makes those RF transmitter and receiver more do with the Arduino. This wireless transmitter and receiver will operate at 4:33 mega hubs so they can easily fit into a breadboard and work well with microcontrollers to create a very simple wireless beetle. Since these are only transmitters they will only work communicating data one way; you would need two pairs of different frequencies to act as a transmitter or receiver.

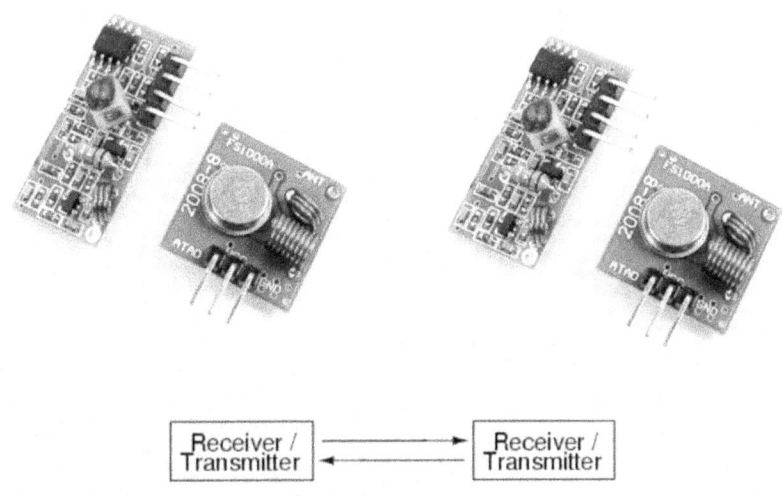

In this project I will explain to you the complete guide for the RF 4:33 megahertz transmitter and receiver model. We will explain this for you how it works and we'll show you how to work with the Arduino. The 4:33 maker has been used on a wide variety of applications that require wireless control. These models are very cheap and you can use them with any microcontroller model specification. This model is a specification for transmitter frequency range for thirty three point ninety two megahertz input voltage three to 12 volt. So this model really trusts me up to 90 meters in an open area for receiver frequency rings for thirty three point ninety two major holes working matter S.K. input voltage five whole. They often use the antenna to increase the effectiveness of your wireless communication. A simple wire will do the trick.

HARDWARE REQUIREMENTS AND WIRING TO AN ARDUINO

Later start building the project let them see what hardware components are required for this project. Who really knows. RF 4:33 megahertz receiver and transmitter wiring to an agreement. And this project receiver and transmitter modules are connected separately who do Arduino boards. First let's see the connection of a receiver module which is an Arduino, the receiver data ping connected to win number 11 of the Arduino Globus.

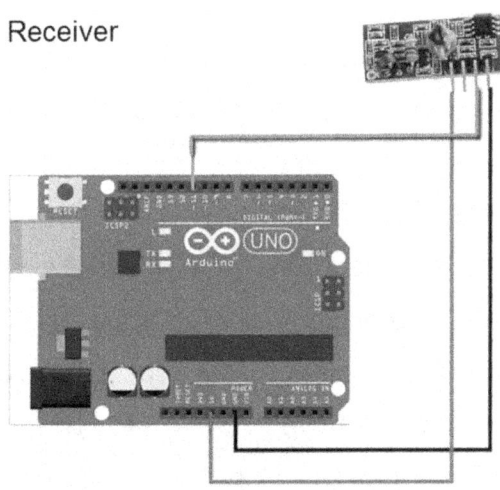

Connect it to clone BTC to fight up our real hard transmitter or do the transmitter beat up when it's connected to one of the Arduino and the ground is connected to clone the PC is connected to the fiber of the Arduino. Please note that there are two separate notes for each module.

CODE RF 433MHZ RECEIVER MODULE TO AN ARDUINO

Now let us see the complete code for this project. Start the ivy before starting the code. We need to add the library to this project. You can download the library in the resource tab. Once you download the fine, let's see how to add in the Arduino ID, download the Radiohead library and give the Radiohead library installed the Radiohead library in your Arduino. We have added the Radiohead library in our Arduino ID. Now we start Arduino ID. The Radiohead library is great and it works with almost all our models. Now let's see the program for the receiver circuit. The library as a dark edge is not actually used but it is needed for completion. The serial dont begin with about three top 9600 is only for the debugging mode and if the driver is not initialized for any reason it will print in the serial monitor in isolation feed coming to quite low Funston.

```
RF433_Receivers
#include <RH_ASK.h>
#include <SPI.h>
RH_ASK driver;

void setup()
{
    Serial.begin(9600);
    if (!driver.init())
        Serial.println("init failed");
}

void loop()
{
    uint8_t buf[12];
    uint8_t buflen = sizeof(buf);
    if (driver.recv(buf, &buflen))
    {
        int i;
        Serial.println("Device is ready");
```

We have been clear and everybody able with size to this will start the receiver PLL. You must do this before you can receive any messages the size of Ponson will calculate the buffer size and is stored in the variable the plane. Now let us come to the if condition did driver not receive Ponson accept that too argument above and both Foreland. Here we are printing the message. The device is really on the receive the message will be printed on the screen that received the message from another Arduino will be printed. Here now compain and upload this code into the Arduino.

CODE RF 433MHZ TRANSMITTER MODULE TO AN ARDUINO

Now let us see the code for the transmitter module here. The white set up concern is almost similar to the receiver, more letting us come to the white loop and send the message which we are sending to the receiver module as defined under the message variable hello world. We are calculating the length of that three using SD or Funston; the Dreiberg dart sent by Ponson will send the message with the given land. Then you define Ponson Dreiberg dot it back and will block and wait until a amasses is available from the receiver. Now compile and upload this code into the Arduino.

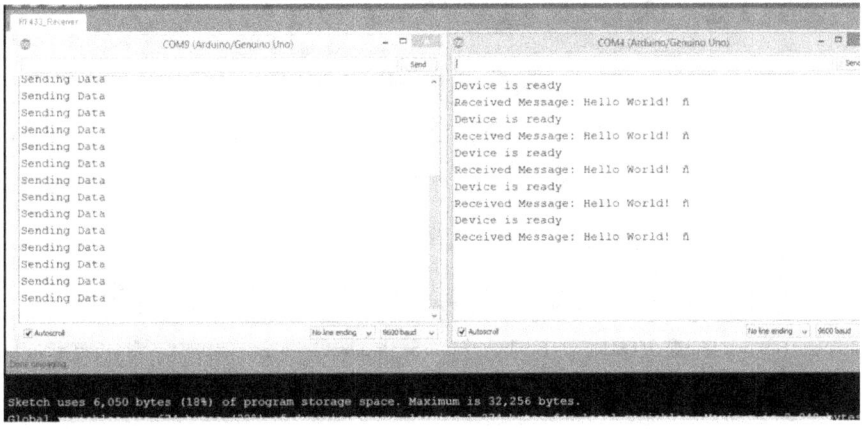

Let us see the real time demonstration of this project in this project. The transmitter is sending a message hello world to the receiver via radio frequency. These messages are displayed in the serial monitor from the receiver. Here you can see the message in your Arduino IAB ID serial monitor. You need to have some realistic expectations when using this model. They work very well. When the receiver and transmitter are close to each other if you separate them too far you will lose the communication. The communication range will be ready. It depends on how much voltage that you are supplying to your transmitter. Radio frequency noise in your environment. And if you are using an external antenna.

ARDUINO CAPACITIVE TOUCH SENSOR

This little DTP 2:23 is the Arduino capacity that is used in this project. The device uses your body as part of the circuit. When you touch a sensor pad the capacitance of the circuit is changed at. That detected a change in capacitance resulting in the output of the space.

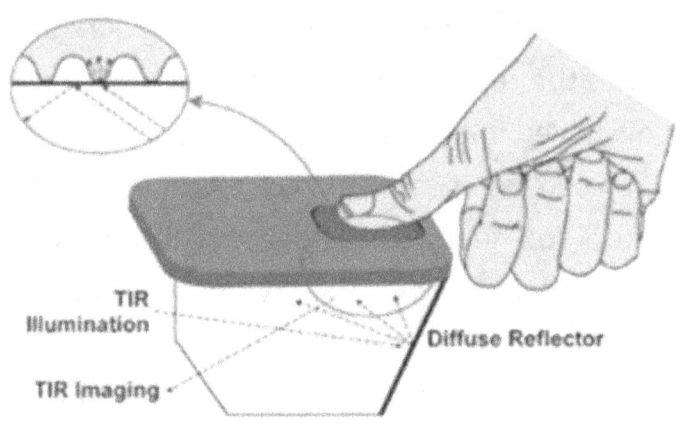

When we first got this I had an idea to make a touch sensitivity like who is doing this project. We need a really more dual core switching recurring. Let see the pin out for DTP 2:23 the digital capacitive sensor like a lot of the sensors out there. This is a three pin sensor. This sensor provides power ground and monitors the output Lakers start building the project. Let us see the hardware components required for this project. Arduino DTP does 23 better touch sensor relay lamp jumper wires breadboard wiring to an Arduino. Now let us connect the dots sensor Well well three. As you can see in the circuit diagram connect the relay more to the sensor and the lamb with no.

CODING AND REAL

Literacy the complete code for this project. This program provides an output we are cereal monitor indicating whether the sensor is pressed or not. The relay is connected to the Arduino PIN number three and the city has been connected to number two. The city here refers to the capacity of the sensor under the white set up Funston. We are enabling the sensor pin as input to receive input when the user touches the capacity of those sensors and the relay as an output under the bright Funston we are reading that sensor value and printing on the serial meter. Now if the received value is high it will bring. Touched on the Seattle monitor screen. And that really gets on the what in a reverse are that passing law in really means that it will trigger high and blow the bird. And now let's see the other condition. If you're not touching the sensor it will display the message not just on the bulb will be off. Now compile the code and upload to the adrenal desk job. I do not cage.

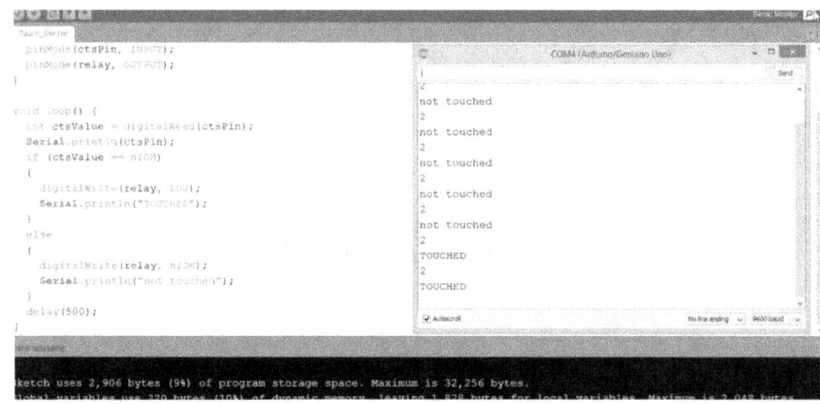

Once you have uploaded this cage, open your CVN monitor and touch the scene said bad while looking at the monitor. You can see the output when you touch the sensor. It really displays the message and also the lamp gets activity.

GETTING TO KNOW ABOUT THE BIO

Done your fingerprint sensor into a biometric toggle switch. This is my first fingerprint sensor project to reuse those fingerprints and recognize the user being accessed with the biometric system and was curious if we would use a fingerprint to turn on our device.

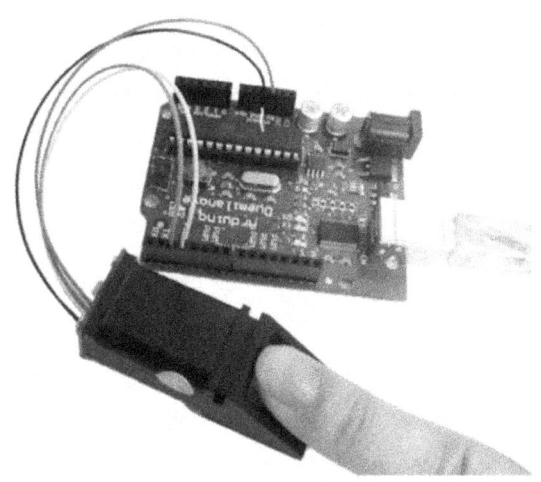

Let's talk about the fingerprint sensor and indeed the security of our project with biometrics. This all in one optical fingerprint sensor will make I think fingerprint detection and verification. Super simple this model is typically used in say there is a high powered DSP team that does that image rendering calculation feature finding and searching connect to any microcontroller or system with LCD and send packets of data to big Porto's detect Prince hash and search. You can also in all new fingers directly up to 162 fingerprints can be stored in the onboard flash memory. There is a real ality in the link that lights up during a photo. So you can't know that it is working. We like this particular sensor because not only is it easy to use. It also comes with fairly straightforward Windows software that makes testing the more simple. You can even enroll using the software and see an image of the fingerprint on your computer screen. This sensor is by far the best fingerprint sensor you can get.

WINDOWS SOFTWARE HARDWARE REQUIREMENTS AND WIRING TO AN ARDUINO

Building a project like this sees what hardware components are quiet. I know are 3 0 5 fingerprints and so waiting to end our dream.

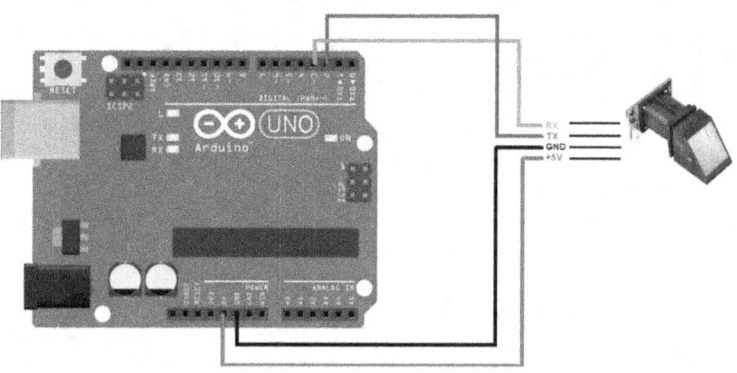

Now let Us take the fingerprints answer to our Greenall who I think that bring the Arduino simply take the following as shown in the circuit diagram connecting the module up. It's pretty straightforward hardware connections fingerprint sensor interfacing to the Arduino Arik Spin of the Pinga plane to Arduino of our expense zero the exception to the Arduino all DXP one grauen to go DCC. Do I know why Paul's software was set up? Once we have all the parts together we need to install the software that will make the fingerprint sensor module in rolling searching and seizing that image of the fingerprint in the system. This software you can download from the resource tab.

DOWNLOAD AND INSTALL THE WINDOWS SOFTWARE APPLICATION

Now let us see how the fingerprint sensor model works. The basic idea is to make the fingerprint sensor to act as a switch. We are making an intelligent switch that can only be activated by you registered users. This could be helpful if you want to personalize your electrical devices. Now we will make a simple fingerprint project starting with the ID and upload the blank code to your Arduino. Please note that the blank SKG wants the word for the make up read to you based on renos like the not on the micro.

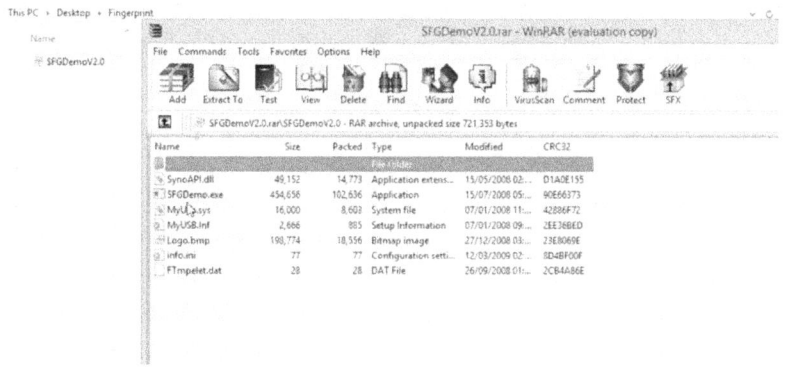

Open the demo software and then start rolling the user's fingerprint in rolling your finger. Using Windows software there are two requirements for using the optical fingerprint sensor. First you will need to install fingerprints. That means assigning IDs to each print so you can read them later.

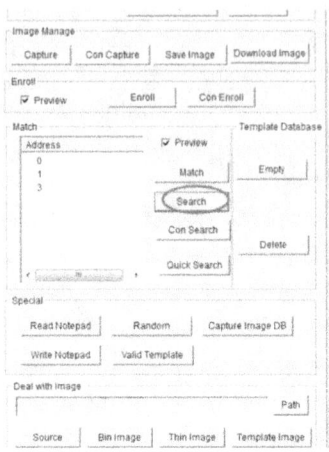

Once you have indoor all your prints you can easily search the sensor asking it to identify which ID is currently POTA crap. You can enroll using the Windows software or with the angriness gauge enrolling new users with Windows. The easiest way to enroll a new fingerprint is to use the software that interface or test software is Windows only but you only need to use it once to enroll to get the pink print. You want to store in the margin First up you want to connect the sensor to the computer via a USP CDR converter. The easiest way to do this is to connect it directly to the USP or serial converter in the Arduino to do this.

You will need to upload a blank skitch. This one works well for traditional adrenals like the UN and the make up wire up the sensor as described in this cage comments after uploading this case since the sensor wires are so thin and short we strip the wire a bit and melted some folded on so it made contact. But you may want to shoulder the wires to the header or similar. If you are not getting good contact when you plug in the power you should see the red Elodie blink to indicate the sensor is working.

ENROLLING FINGERPRINT USING WINDOWS SOFTWARE

Start of the SAGD more software and click Open Device From the bottom left corner select the compost used by the Arduino and press OK when done you should see the following. With the Blue sexist message and some device the status in the bottom corner you can change the boundary in the bottom left hand corner. As well as the security level, how sensitive it is. But we suggest leaving those alone until you have everything running and you want to experiment. They should be forced to be the 7600 bowed and security level 3.

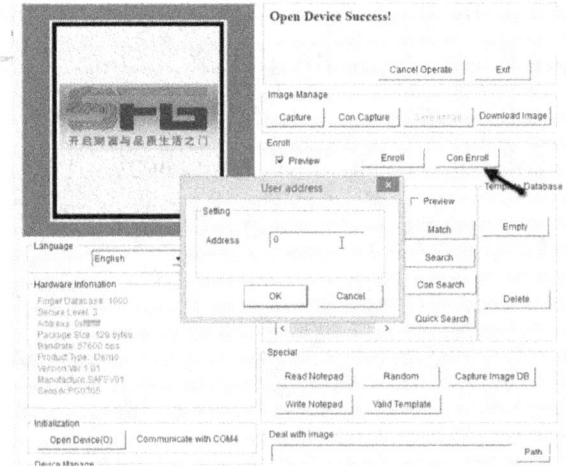

So set them if they are wrong let's in all new fingers click the preview check box and press the button next to it. Gone in all means continuous in all which you may want to do if you have many fingers to enroll. When the box comes up, enter in the ID you want to use. You can use up to 162 ID numbers. The software will ask you to press the finger to the sensor. You can then see a preview if you click the preview checkbox of the fingerprint. You will then have to repeat the process to get a second clean print.

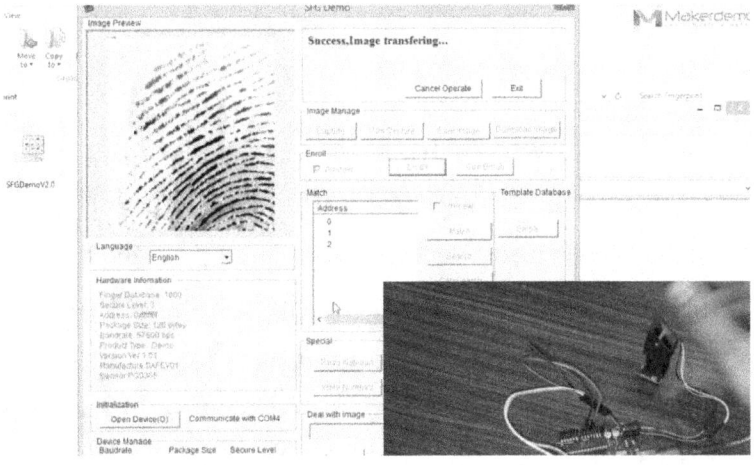

Use the same Pingo on success you will get a notice if there is a problem such as bad print or image. You will have to do it again searching with the software. Once you have the finger in all it is a good idea to do a quick test to make sure it can be found in the database. Click on the search button on the right hand side. When prompted press are different or same Pinga to the sensor. If it is the same Pinga you should get a match with the ID number if it is not a finger in the database. You will get a failure notice.

TESTING THE ENROLLED FINGERPRINT USING ARDUINO IDE

Whiting for use with Arduino Once you have destroyed dozens of you can now use it within ASCII to verify a fingerprint. We really do require a sense of disconnect the R X and X Y S and T are x y in the digital 3 and the THYR to digital too. You can't change dispenses later but for now use the departments in the circuit diagrams. We have connected the wires directly into the Arduino. However this does not work well because the wires are so thin and they don't mean contact. You should shoulder Tikker solid core wires to each wire to make good contact.

It is normal for the sensor to blink the read Elodie quickly once powered up so that the LNB will be up until you have started to request data from the next download. The other fruit fingerprints since the library from the resource tab to download the zip file in the resource tab and rename the compressed folder and fruit underscore fingerprint check that the underscore fingerprint Folder contains fruit underscore fingerprint dot CTP and ADAP fruit underscore fingerprint dark edge place to underscore fingerprint library folder. Your libraries slash folder. You may need to create the library's subfolder if it is not for slavery. Restocked your ID. Once you have restarted you should be able to select the file then.

Examples. Then under a duffer and the school fingerprint example Skitch upload it to your audience. As usual, open up the cereal monitor at 9600 baud and when prompted. Place your finger against the sensor that is really in all you will see the following the confidence easiest call number from 0 to 255. That indicates how good of a match this is, how your beat. Please note that if it matches at all that means the sensor is pretty confident. So you don't have to pay attention to the confidence number unless it makes sense for high security applications. If you want to have a more detailed report. Change the loop to run fingerprint ID instead of get fingerprints. Yes Hunsdon that will give you a detailed report of exactly what the sensor is detecting at each point of the search process.

ENROLLING AND SEARCHING FINGERPRINT USING ARDUINO IDE

Enrolling with the Arduino we did put together a simple cage for rolling a newfangled via Arduino. It is not as easy to use as the Windows program but it does work. Read the fine examples of the fruit finger print in a sketch and uploaded to your Arduino. Please use the same wiring when you open up the CELL monitor.

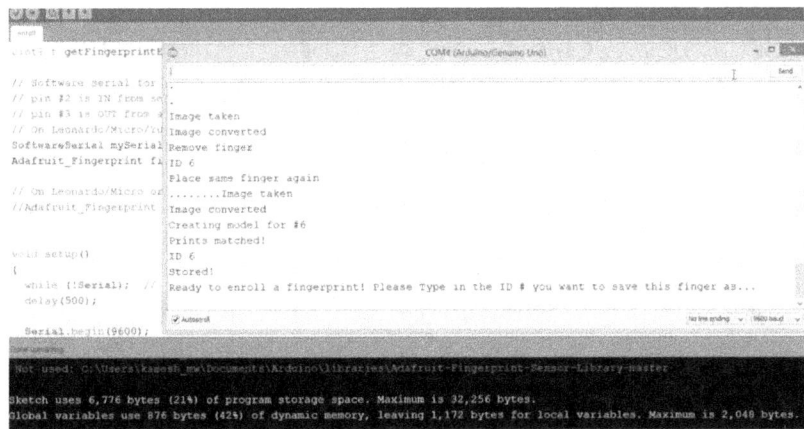

It will ask you to type that ID to enroll. Use the box on top to type in and number and click on saying. Then go to the in process as indicated when it has successfully installed a finger. It will print stored. Don't forget to do a search just when you are done enrolling to make sure it is all good.

INTRODUCTION TO ARDUINO MICROCONTROLLER

I welcome everyone for this wonderful cause on an industrial level programming in order no I.D. based on order, no. You know, development both in this course, we will not be using any of the inbuilt library and header files that are available in the order no IBC. Instead of that, we will be configuring the registers of the microcontroller that is available in the ordinal, you know, development mode. And we will be writing our own user defined functions for accessing the peripherals, as well as for establishing the communication protocols that are supported by the same microcontroller and the microcontroller that is available in the ordinal, you know, borders. I've got three, two, eight and in this project, we are just going to discuss different inference and communication protocols supported by this microcontroller. First and foremost, peripheral GPI was useful for interfacing input and output devices to the microcontroller, and we have three different DPA reports.

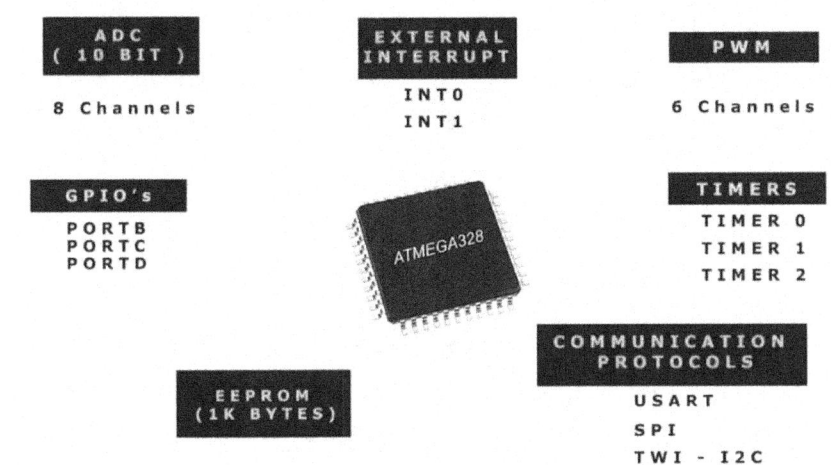

What we would see on would be in this microcontroller and the next peripherals timeless. It has three different timers. They are timer, zero timer, one on payment, two and further. It has an ABC module, which is useful for converting analog signals into digital signals, and this module has six different channels in the microcontroller. All the timers from timer zero two Timer two are having at least two open combat channels, through which we can then be doubling segments of that quiet frequency and due to cycle totally. We have six different channels for generating BWB. Then we have two different external interrupt channels through which we can enter the processor using external sources, and we have one kilobyte of internal E from what it's useful for storing non-volatile data while functioning. There are few communication protocols that are supported by this microcontroller. They are used at the universal synchronous asynchronous receiver transmitter. Yes, a serial interface, which is a synchronous communication and PWI, which is nothing but intel integrated communication or two way interface. And that is all about the peripheral structure and communication protocols that are supported by this at Mega 7:57 microcontroller and on from the next project, we will try to access the very pulse of the microcontroller by programming the microcontroller, as well as we will try to interface other devices to the microcontroller using the communication protocol supported by this microcontroller.

FEATURES OF ARDUINO MICROCONTROLLER

We know that the microcontroller available in our Arduino borders at Megahed, three to eight. And in this project, we are just going to discuss some of the features of this upcoming upgrade to a microcontroller. So these are the features that you must know before buying any microcontroller. Let's get started. So this at minus three to eight, is an eight bit microcontroller, which means all the internal register arrangement of this microcontroller will be only in the form of a bit Swype. So we must give our data but one of eight bits to this microcontroller. And secondly, it hasn't 32 kilobytes, last memory. This last memory is nothing but the program memory of the microcontroller. So this 7:57 can hold a program of 32 kilobytes. And we have one kilobyte of Ebro, so this from memory is useful for storing non-volatile data while the microcontroller is running.

FEATURES

And we have two kilobytes of RAM, and we just store the data that the microcontroller uses while the program is being executed. And the maximum frequency at which this microcontroller can run is 30 megahertz, it can provide an external crystal oscillator of 20 maggots to this microcontroller. So that's all about the basic features for any microcontroller that you must know before buying a microcontroller. And we will see the benefits of this microcontroller in that upcoming little.

PIN LAYOUT & PORT STRUCTURE OF ARDUINO MICROCONTROLLER

We are just going to discuss the bin layout and boat sector of development boats. And we know that the microcontroller that is available on our no development bonus at Mega three to eight, which isn't on tape and we are microcontrollers. And the first happiness reset bin of the microcontroller and this bin, when it is put into law, this pin will automatically restart the program of our microcontroller from the beginning and the this is the vehicle for one microcontroller through which we must provide a power supply of 3.3 to 5.5. All unrepentantly is nothing but the analog business that is gimmicky. This is used as an ASN power supply pin for the analog to digital converter model of our microcontroller and print and print. On this are the governments through which we must provide the ground to the microcontroller. And Bin

21 was the analog reference bin, and we just use it as a reference or pitch for converting analog signals into digital signals using the ADC model of auto microcontroller and Penylan printing, or the Crystal Oscillator pins through which we can provide that frequency to the microcontroller using external crystal oscillator. The maximum clock that we can provide to these microcontrollers is 20 megahertz. And next, we're just going to the CD board structure of this microcontroller. And the first to put this would be on this podcast totaling eight points, starting from zero to PB seven. And as I said, we are just going to use PB six, some PB seven in our microcontroller for connecting external crystal oscillators in our development mode. So we are totally having six points in the sport, but this zero 2p Wi-Fi and the pin number starting from 14 to 19 and the next report to support see this sport has totally seven points, starting from zero to PCs.

PIN LAYOUT   ATMEGA328 - 28 PIN

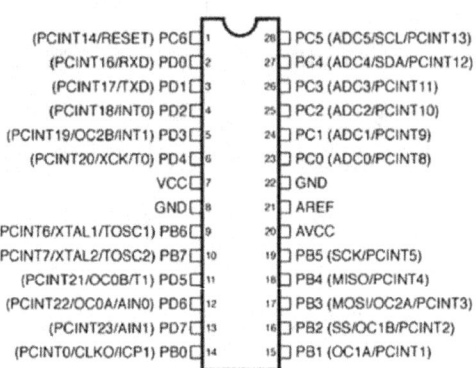

And this business is meant for research purpose, and that is why this podcast totally six points that this piece is the rate of PC and the pin number starting from 23 to 28 on the third portal Sport B and this bolt has totally eight points, starting from pretty zero to seven, and the pin numbers are from 10 to 2.6 and then from 11 to 13. You can see these are the nailed on board structure of this microcontroller. This microcontroller has three ports, four and three. And in this course, we are just going to program this Arduino board using register level programming. Right for that, we will be using only these big nodes and physically in what order number you will be seeing these nodes highlighted in red and these notes that are highlighted in red will be useful for us while we are building the hardware side for demonstration. But while programming, we will be using one of these pin nodes unprotected off this microcontroller.

HARDWARE & SOFTWARE USED IN THIS COURSE PART - 1

We're just going to discuss the hardware and software components that we are going to use and what this course is. The development board that we are going to use this ordinance, you know, development board. Andy, the microcontroller available on this development board is nothing but bigotry to a B if you are a microcontroller. And through this power that you can power this alternate development mode using external told one of this. And we have a 16 maggots external, still isolated character to be attracted to it. It's full of little bits. And through this USB-C port, you can connect this alternate development board to your PC USB port, but programming this microcontroller and this is the reset button of the auto note development mode, which is connected to the reset button of the three two eight.

HARDWARE

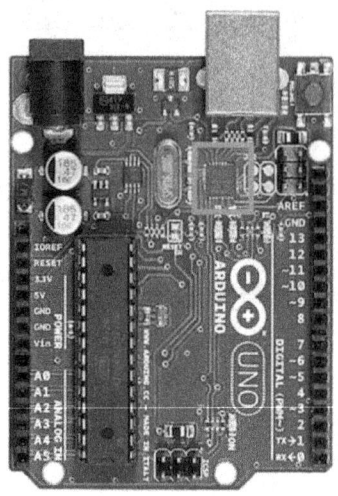

And this is the on board I a programmer with this usage for loading the flats onto the microcontroller. And we have one on board, al-Libbi, which is currently 2D digital, 13 of no development on this digital print 13 is nothing but the Port B file of the Army two eight, which is nothing but b bb five will not be. I got these two eight microcontrollers. And regarding the softer parts, we are just going to use it for programming this microcontroller. And regarding the software bots, we are just going to use the audio iby for programming this microcontroller.

HARDWARE & SOFTWARE USED IN THIS COURSE PART - 2

We will discuss the hardware components required for this code on star level programming. You'll notice both. So the only software required is ordinal IBM, and we will try to download and install the software in the next project, and in this project we will discuss about the hardware requirements for this course and we will keep on updating this course with new projects on once we are there, the course with new projects, you will get it like this. And after receiving that, you can buy the hardware components for those projects. But no, this is the basic requirement for this course. And I even suggest you buy these components before starting this course. Initially, you just want to know your development board will be cable. And then we need firemen in need of any color with authority that stutters. Then we want a common cat seven segment display with an open water system. And we need to push buttons and 210 km systems. And then we need 16 cross to alphanumeric LCD displays, along with a 10 kms variable resistor.

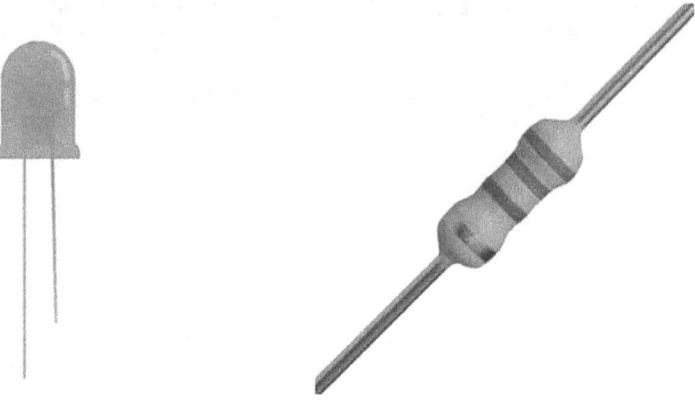

Then we want to hit zero for a Bluetooth module. And then we want the 2014 04 I2C from ICI along with 210km sisters. You can buy the 04 model if it is available, or you can buy this separately and you can build this. So that's all about the hardware components required for this course, and a list for those components is provided in the download section of this video. So click on the download button below the description of this video to see the list of components required for this course.And the registered level programming course in order no. And I'm assuming that I will keep on updating the force with onboard interfaces, saying the next project.

DOWNLOADING ARDUINO IDE SOFTWARE

We just discussed the hardware and software components that are required for this registered level programming course in ordinal. And in this project, I'm just going to show you how you can download the ordinal IBD for what I see. Go to Google and type in Padrino. And you will get this order, no doubt CC site anacondas or no hyphen software link. You will get to this download speed, scroll down a little bit, and here you can see download the audio no I.D.. This one is the latest order no I.D. software that this wasn't one point eight point twelve. And here you can see this is for Windows.

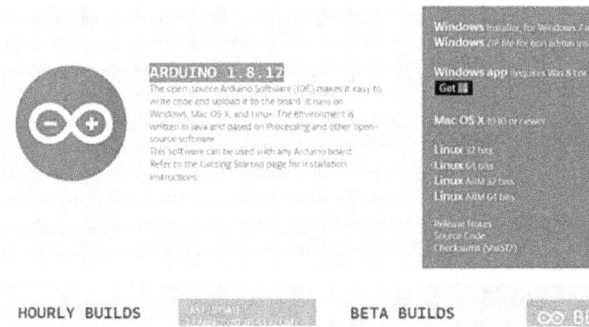

And this one's for Mac and this one's for Linux and the installer as an offline installer. So you can download the installer and then you can easily install the software to your PC. Now when clicking on it. And in the next bit, you can just download.

INTRODUCTION TO ARDUINO IDE

We are just going to see how we can set up our order no I.D. for programming. Initially, connect the order number to your PC, USB port through USB cable. Once connected, open the order no I.D.. Among all the members of Quest, this order is the simplest one that you need not do anything other than selecting the board and the board requirement. And you can see there are two functions initially. This void setup is useful for writing the configurable items of the program, which needs to be executed only once in the program.

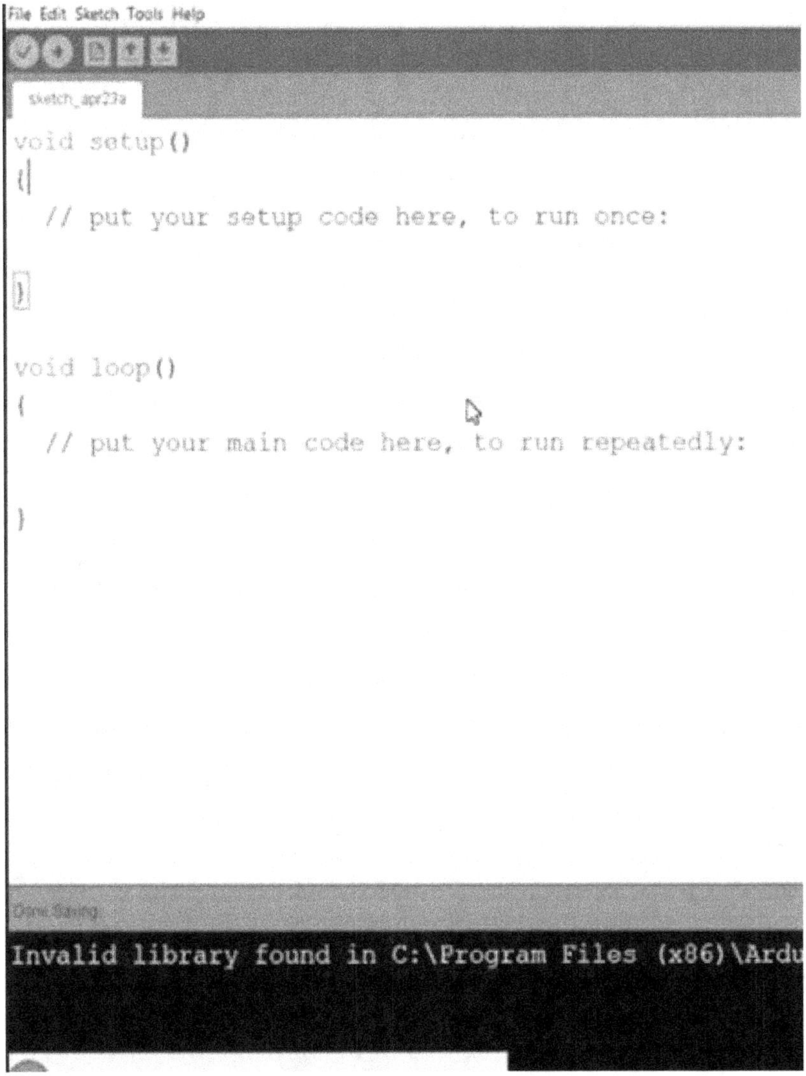

```
File Edit Sketch Tools Help

sketch_apr23a
void setup()
{
  // put your setup code here, to run once:

}

void loop()
{
  // put your main code here, to run repeatedly:

}

Done Saving
Invalid library found in C:\Program Files (x86)\Ardu
```

And this wide loop is nothing but an infinite loop in the program, which is used for writing the logic that needs to be executed again and again until the microcontroller is stopped. These are the differences between these two functions and know what the final unsaved project in any of your locations, according to you on this. After that, Go to the toll stop under that water board and select this order, no ordinance, no, you know, one selecting the board again, go to the Port tab and duty required port that is connecting to the new development board. You can see it near the WSJ.com number. This order no ordering, no you know, name will be available. Click on that. And after that, under the programmer, select the order no ISP. And that's our order.

FEATURES OF ARDUINO IDE

We are just going to see how we can set up our audio I.D. program. And then we will be discussing what is a seated monitor in IBD. And we are going to try to get some data for this even more in depth from the moment no matter the controller. Let's get started. So once you have done with the downloading and installation of the audio, I'd open the audio iby and then click on file. No, no. The new file has been opened the on file and then we can say we just want to save your new project. What are the respective folder as well? And then give us the spectrum name and then click on to and you can see there are two functions of setup on wide loop. So initially, if you take anything but a program, there are two parts. One is the one thing configurable parts unknown, mixed to see repeatable executable parts. So one thing configurable parts are nothing but the programming line that makes you executed one day once the lifespan of the program. So, for example, if they want to configure a particular business input or output, that needs to be done only once, right? So those kinds of things will be written in the wide setup, but this name function for writing them one thing one program will pass.

```
salsa
void setup()
{
    // put your setup code here, to run once:

}

void loop()
{
    // put your main code here, to run repeatedly:

}
```

Regarding this, why blue? But is it nothing but an infinite loop or a super low, which is useful for writing these repeatable executable segments of the program? So these repeatable executable segments of a program, it's nothing but the programming line that needs to be executed again and again until the lifetime of the microcontroller. So this is the logic actually like so every microcontroller program will be having a logic that needs to be executed again and again. So those kinds of lines must be written inside this wide loop. So whatever is written inside, this wide loop will be executed again and again and again and again until the microcontroller stops. So initially, when the program starts, the execution comes over here and it will execute the programming language that is available and league wide setup. So we just want to. Configurable items are one thing. Configurable programming lines are not executing all domains, present indebtedness, void setup. The program executes and enters into this void loop on this wide loop. Well, we keep on executing again and again and again and again until these microcontrollers stop them. It will never be left from this loop until the microcontrollers are turned off. So this is the normal program execution flow of an embedded program and now learn about the serial monitor. So once you are done with the compiling, connect to it Automate Development Board to your PC, USB port, the USB cable, and then you can click on this button for offloading the program to you. What is below, you know? You can see. We can see the program has been successfully uploaded to what ordinary you know, and click on this whole tab and you can see the port connector for the ordinary United Country if it is not selected. You just wanted to select that and then select the program or the Niobe, and then you just wanted to select the bottle or the audience, you know. And if you are using any of the boards like Nano or Chrome Mini or Mega, you just want to select the respective mode and you can see the sequence you save. This gets to a particular location. And here is a certain icon called serial monitor on the top right corner to conduct, and you can see a window popping up on this serial monitor transmitting, but that window. But it's useful for displaying data that is coming from the serial port of the or the no microcontroller. The serial monitor is mainly used for displaying disks from overuse, the written program, or mainly it is used for deepening the use of it and program in the Abbey, which is a special feature which is not available on any other platform, but it is available in order. No.

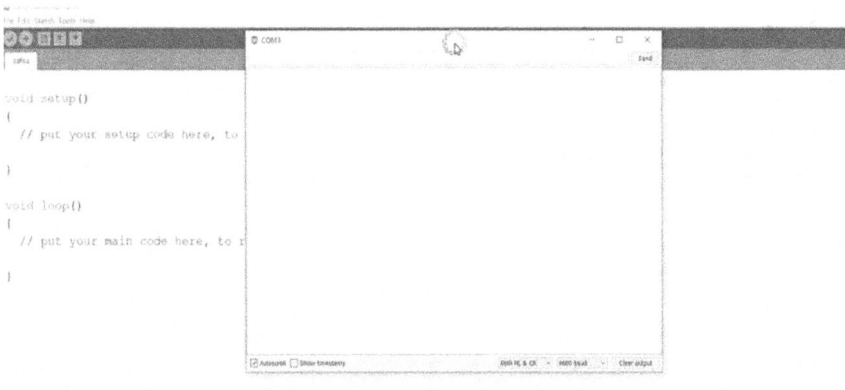

So you can make use of the Syrian monitoring each and every program of use or displaying data, as well as for debugging what you sort of program. So let's try to send some data from our program for the serial monitor. I have already connected the automated, you know, development board to my PC USB port to use the cable. And you can see. This is a serial port business digital pen, one of the departments of serial port and digital dealer. Did you see what happened off the serial port on these two bins or internally connected to the USB port of the ordinary, you know, microcontroller? So you need not make any other further connections for communicating with DC didn't want to get it. You just want to connect the USB cable from the USB port on the PC today or you know, that's enough now.

HARDWARE

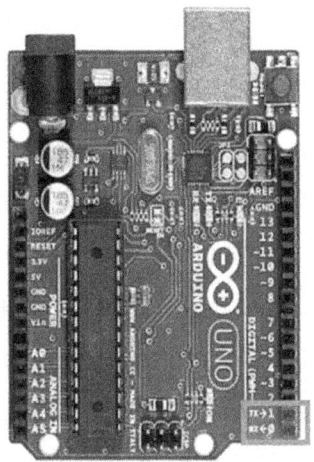

So let's see some of the internal functions of ordinary IAB, but it's available for serial communication. So these are the functions. So the same functions we will be using for serial protocol, but that we will be seeing a beep. But here we will just know what are dysfunctions. So for insulating the serial port of the no microcontroller, we just want to use this serial dot to begin a slowly going saving ward setup. So this is a one time executable part. We just want to see it put one in once in the lifetime of the program. So I am writing this line inside the white setup serial dot begin, and this function raises one parameter of just nothing. But we both require the communication between the serial monitor and the ordinal microcontroller serial port. So generally we will be using 9600 the or we have several options, but the standard is 9600. I'm using the 9600. Our next thing is cereal, dot, print, so this is useful for printing data. So this even wanted to. So coming into the wide loop, I'm just going to say. Cereal, dot, print. And some cleaning. Academy, so after this, I'm just going to give a delay of one second. So this is the internal debate that is available in the order, no idea, but just in milliseconds, so a thousand milliseconds is nothing but one second. So in this program, you can see once the program and some starts, it comes to the wired setup and it will be you need to listen to the serial port of the microcontroller with 9600 boundaries. And after that, it comes into the wide loop and it will bend the data, or it will send the data from the serial port that is some training academy after sending the data it will be waiting for once again and after executing this line. But as to particularly this last line again, it will be going into the fast lane and it will continue this training academy. So this process continues and it will be executing again and again and again and again, and it will be printing the same data until they might to let it stop. So this is the execution of the program. No one combines this. Then I'm uploading this get to the ordinary, you know, the program has been successfully uploaded now. Click on this icon for opening the serial monitor. And you just want to set the border over here, you can see nine thousand six under the default. You can do any other border. Accordingly, you just want to say that in the program. I know so I will be nine thousand hundred, we can see you have some training academy is being green again and again.

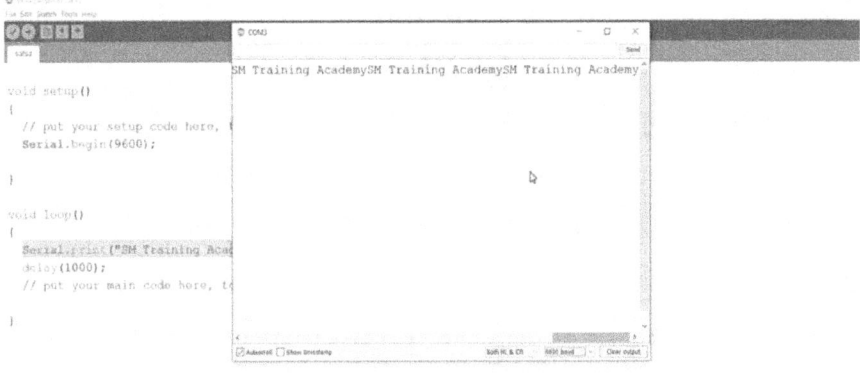

And the next the function is you're going to see serial Dortmund Alan, which is nothing but. Let's demonstrate that. So at this point, Ellen Johnson will transmit the same data, but after the data, it will be sending commands for Kerry and written as well as New Line. So this training academy will be printed in the new line one after the other. Now again, I'm compiling this kit. Now I'm getting this icon for uploading the sketch to the order. No, you know, I'm opening the city monitor. You can see some training academy sentences being printed on the new line again and again within the time span of one second. And you can see these three functions right, available and brief. It's also serial communication protocol phantoms. So this serial right available agreed-upon is specially meant for serial port of the ordinal microcontroller, and this is meant for writing letters to a particular device like, for example, in and out of it. But here we will not be using it for, say, not monitoring. We will be most often using this print and in this serial monitor. And remember one thing that this print function is used to for sending character or string of data to this, he didn't want to turn down, send a variable of integer values or any other values today, so he didn't want a monitor. So if you want to send a decimal value to the serial monitor, the only thing you want to know is you just want to pass the abysmal value, for example, a b and then you want to add another parameter that has come out b c. So this will transmit the dismal value 18 to the monitor. So actually, what it does is that it will convert this value 18 ASCII with just a serial parameter data and then it will send that serial monitor when companies get taken. And I'm applauding the program. Now you can see the decimal value A B is being converted to be dissimilar to ASCII, and then it is being printed on this serial monitor. Like this, you can also send the data as well as open data. So he didn't want it, though we got an Intel boss to the serial Brent funds and also one of the things that it will not be followed would be done under Newland command, but it will be printing it again and again in the same line and at the same venue counterparts. The Hicks value and of their value to be a brain function, similar to the data being posted directly to the serial print and billing function. You can also pass a variable of data to the serial incident parental consent for printing the value of the variable to the serial monitor. So for doing that, I'm getting a variable data and I'm giving an integer value eighty nine. So for printing this data, whatever to do this or the only change that I will do this, I will pass the variable over here since I'm parsing integer value to the data variable. I'm just retaining this argument that this decimal so this decimal value will be converted into ASCII before transmitting into the serial monitor. No. I'm comparing this gift and uploading it. You can see the integer value 89 is being put on to the serial monitor.

```
void setup()
{
  // put your setup code here, to run once:
  Serial.begin(9600);
}
char data = 89;
void loop()
{
  Serial.println(data, DEC);
  delay(1000);
  // put your main code here, to run repeatedly:
}
```

Sketch uses 1688 bytes (5%) of program storage space. Maximum is 32256 bytes.
Global variables use 188 bytes (9%) of dynamic memory, leaving 1860 bytes for local variables. Maximum is 2048 bytes.

No, I'm just trying to foster hexadecimal data, for example. Zero, five, six. No, I just want to give you here, folks, so that this will depend on the political monitor. I'm applauding this gets to the ordinary, you know? Only you can see the hexadecimal data for physics is being printed out to be a serial monitor. And if you are passing a character just like this, or if you are passing the screen, you need not give the second argument you can directly Bosnian variable data. But you can see the carpet is being too dependent on the serial monitor. And let's wait a little bit differently. I am buzzing, abysmal data AP. And if I'm giving this X, let's see what is happening. You can see the super data. AP is being converted into one form of talisman and then it is converted to ASCII before transmitting to the monitor. So we are getting the value well over here. Let's cross-check that. So I'm giving a dismal data, AP Benzie, the equal, and it's a dismal data as well. So that is why we are getting well over here. Now you can see this military thing is being built around the decision monitor, so you must be very conscious while you are converting the data into required a full month and you must be passing the correct format of this acknowledgement of the civil print President Lyndon Johnson. And that's all about this. You don't monitor commands. You're going to use military commands, want us to begin, just use the body. And instead, if you can see the import of the order microcontroller and next want to see SEAL Print, which will be printing the data continuously in and sit in and monitor our next one is the serial print alone with just printing the data, along with the areas that are done on Newland command at the end. So these three are the functions that we will be using most often for the serial monitor. Drop the order no I.D. And regarding all these serial functions, we will be seeing that in the serial communication protocol project in the future projects. For now, you just want to remember that there is a thing called deal monitoring or the ABC we can use to know the data from the use of a program, as well as what debugging purposes.

EMBEDDED C REGISTER BIT MANIPULATION TECHNIQUES PART – 1

We are just going to see it deeply over configuration for our microcontroller at three to eight that is available in Arduino Development Board. So in this project, we are just going to see some of the big manipulation logic that is applied for setting and cleaning bits in Nevada internal registries of our microcontroller. So this is a very important picture. So you would not miss any step in this project. And this is common for any register in what microcontroller? What is an output? So what is some signal that the microcontroller gives to the external voice? So any signal that is given by the microcontroller to the external world is called output and examples of output, the basis are you ladies yell CDs and seven segment displays. And what is an input input is some signal that the microcontroller receives from the external world, so anything that is coming from the external source to the microcontroller is called US input. And some examples of input devices are. So it just loses buttons and any kind of sensor. As I said, our microcontroller has an eight bit microcontroller, so all the internal registers of all microcontrollers will be one in the form of eight bits wide.

REGISTER STRUCTURE

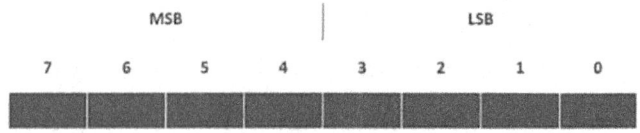

So this is the common thread of this destructive part of one microcontroller starting from zero to seven. So these bits from big zero to three are called us. Yeah, let's be. We're just nothing but these two significant bits and these bits from before two bits. Seven are called us, you must be, which is nothing but the most significant bits. And create a registers that we are going to see for the dpa of the microcontrollers, Bebe Optics data, the Ericsson Register, VORTECS Data Register and Pinnock's Input Print and register. And before that, I just want to remind you to lock the gates that are on an oh so in and get you to see. Zero zero zero zero one zero one zero zero one on one this one and an audit you can see zero zero zero zero one oneone zero one on one one this one.

LOGICAL OPERATIONS

AND				OR		
0	0	0		0	0	0
0	1	0		0	1	1
1	0	0		1	0	1
1	1	1		1	1	1

Any value & zero will give zero
Any value | one will give one

So you just want to remember two things that are of any value and if zero will give us three, zero of any value out of one will give us the result. One.So these two are the important logics that we are going to use for setting and clearing the bits in the Nevada register of the microcontroller. So you just want to remember these two get before entering into the configuration, but. So the first protesters, baby, are that data that I didn't register on this register, it's used for configuring the particular pin of the microcontroller as input output. So this indicates that this is not a constant, and it may be varying depending on reports we are configuring. We have three different ports in our microcontroller, so we have B, B, R B, B, B, R C and D B R B Logistics. You can see B B, R B is having a bit starting from BBC to B seven and BD R C is having seven, but starting from B C02, B, C six and BBC, someone is not available and b b are these having a bet starting from b d d 02 b bb seven.

CONTROL REGISTERS FOR GPIO

Data Direction Register

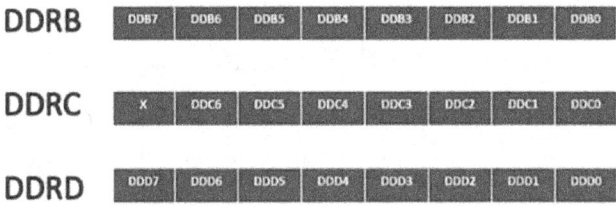

And let's understand how we can configure the business input output using the BP register. That is, if you are writing zero to a particular bit in BP audits, register that particular or that particular pin will be configured as input. And if you are writing one to the corresponding pin, that will configure the business output. So let's understand this There are two methods for sorting or clearing bits in a register that's doing this individual judgment that on the second one is a statement that. So this individual method is used whenever we just want to sit one or two bits of the register and we want to leave the other bits of the registers undisturbed. We will use this eight bit data method for sorting all the bits of the corresponding register. So these are the differences between these two methods, and we will see the individual bits method for treating or clearing the bits in the Cortex register. So initially now we know that if we write one to the pin, that will configure the corresponding bits output. And if we write a veto, it will configure the business input. So let's take the body of buildings that we are just going to configure the port be. If you are going to configure any other port, you just want to take the corresponding B D or C R B. How can you make this b d b zero bit test? Output for that, I just want to write one to the BD be zero type, so that can be done by using this line and can see this line will simply be BBB zero bit off. BD are being understood to be the R B equal to ddrb off one slip of the BBB zero. So let's understand this line initially, let's assume all the bits in the D R B register zero. And this one left the BBC you is nothing but a value that will be zero at the register. So its value will be zero zero zero zero zero zero zero one.

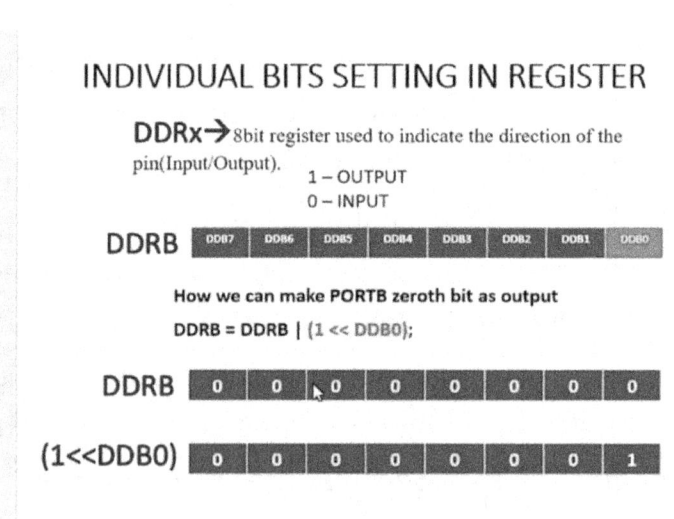

So when they perform our operation of these two registers, anyone who can see zero zero will give me zero zero will give me zero one. This zero one will give me the third one and the result we are storing in the B B R B register. So now the value of B R B registers zero zero zero zero zero zero zero one. So now you can see this d d b zero to set and it's configured as output. So this is how you can set up a register and you can configure the penis output in DV addicts register. And similarly, this person can be certain like this that instead of writing BD R or B equal to bdrbf of one looks off of d d b zero. You can write brbr equal to one left of BBB zero, both having the same meaning. So you can neglect this and be done again. Similarly, if I want this d d b one bit also configured as output, I can just type B, D or B article to one that looks out of BBB zero and then out of one that looks off of BD B one. So this line will set BTB zero and D D B one. Bits of d d are really just configuring these to princess output like this, you can perform as many auto presents in a single line as possible. And if you want to make all this, four bits from BBB zero two d d b three as output I can drive d d r b, all equal to one of the top BBB zero r of one look to the BBB one auto one of BBB to R of one left of Dot BBB three.

INDIVIDUAL BITS SETTING IN REGISTER

DDRx → 8bit register used to indicate the direction of the pin(Input/Output).

1 – OUTPUT
0 – INPUT

DDRB | DDB7 | DDB6 | DDB5 | DDB4 | DDB3 | DDB2 | DDB1 | DDB0 |

How we can make PORTB zeroth bit as output

DDRB |= (1 << DDB0);

Similarly if I make DDB0,DDB1,DDB2,DDB3 as output

DDRB |= (1 << DDB0) | (1 << DDB1) | (1 << DDB2) | (1 << DDB3);

So this line will set all the bits from BBB 0.80 B3 and we will be getting all the princess output. And if I want to make this bit of input, we know that we just want to clear the speed irrespective of the current value that it is having. We just want to clear this bit without disturbing all the remaining bits in the register. So an individual which means that we will want to set the corresponding bit leaving all the bits of the register undisturbed. So that can be done by using this line D, D or B equal to be the R B Amberson of negation of one, looks have to be b zero. So this will clear d dd b zero value irrespective of the current value available in the BBB zero. Let's understand this line. Let's assume the initial value of d d r b to be zero zero zero zero zero one. I'm just purposefully assigning this value as one and the one left off BBB zero will give the value zero zero zero zero zero zero zero one.

And negation of this value, we will be getting all these zeros as one on ones zeros in this register that as result of this negation of one zero will give us one one one one one one one zero. And now when they are built, the store value will be nuggets and one lifts of BBB zero value. You can see all these values will be the same as available in the DVD register as we are performing an operation of that -- with one. So any value under one will give me the same value that is important zero here. It will give me zero here. If it does one, I will get one here and you can see all the values that are available from seven to one, but in the arbitrage instead it is available over here and here you can see the value was zero. So anything under pressure zero will give me the result to feel whatever value that is present here will be cleared. So this is how the D advisor the stock will be holding the value zero zero zero zero zero zero zero zero at the end. Does this DB zero value clear using this line? You can also simplify the slain Asper this BD instead of, I think, b r b equal to B B R B Amberson, and it gets enough one left of BBB zero. You can rip d d r b Amberson equal to linear and off one look of d d b zero. And similarly, if you want this bit also to be configured as input, I just want to clear this bit also that can be done using the statement. B, D or B Amberson, equal to negation of one of the top BTB zero AmbersonN'Guessan and one left the BBB one like this, you can perform at many of our prisons in a single line for clearing, but in a register. So if you want to make all this bring us input from zero to GDP three, I just want to clear all these four bits remaining which we will leave. Understood. Let's see. This line will do this right. That is d d r b Amberson equal to negation of one lift of tough d d b zero and often against another one left the top rated B one and of negation of one left the top D d b two. And of course, no one left and stuff d d b three.

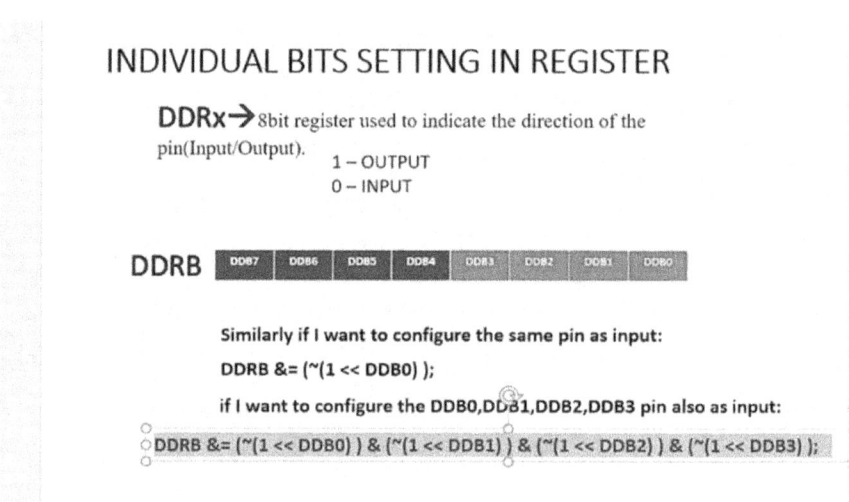

So this line will clear all the bits from D, d b 02 D, D, B three, making that business input. So this is how you can set or clear the bits of the register in. You will bring out 16 microcontrollers using individual bits and let's see the next method that is a bit data setting, but that. So let's take an example for understanding this method also. So you may want to configure all these pins from BBB zero to three princess inputs. And if you want all these pins to be configured as output that's needed before to BBB, seven must be configured as output. What I can do is I just want to write one to it, and I just want to clear all this or that. I can probably do a bit of binary data directly to the BBB b register so that I can write B.V. or be equal to zero be one one one one one zero zero zero zero. So this zero b is representing that. We are providing binary data and these eight bits, if corresponding to the respective. But that is the first step to the BBB seven sevenTypekit of the register under the next operator said two six two and four four three two one one zero. So from the left, the bits will be set from seven to two zero eight bits on the right. So in this order, the books will be certain. So instead of configuring a bit of binary data to the register, we can configure equal and hexadecimal values for this binary data so far, representing this binary data in the form of hexadecimal. We just want to change this zero bit to direct. And then we just want to split these eight bits into the orbit that was before us. It must be next to this LSP. And then you can see this is the table for converting binary data in two equal to hexadecimal. So this one one one one one in binary is Representative Jeff Hexadecimal and this zero zero zero zero representatives zero. It's not that simple. So I can drive B, D or B equal to zero zero, so I can write this, exert its embedded value. Instead of that, eight bit binary data to the D B R B register. So does this table data matter is useful for setting all the eight bits that are registered off a microcontroller? So let's take another example, that is, if you want to configure B the B to B, B B or D D B five princess inputs and all the other princess outputs in B D are below the star. So I just want to set these three values that the second best for the best and first the values are zero, and all the other seven six three one zero must be certain as we know, one is for output and zero is for input. So I can binary data. Zero one one zero zero one zero one one. So the leaders will say to the corresponding business input and once will set the corresponding output. So initially, we just want to configure the binary data onto the register. And then in the next step, we just want to convert this data into ex-servicemen using be able. So for converting that, we just want to replace the zero zero X and then we just want to be able to do what it must to unfold LSP. So the must be one one zero zero one one zero zero in binary is having to exert its total value C and one zero one one is having the ex-serviceman value be. So the hexadecimal value is nothing but b d r b equal to zero CB. So this is the equal index or the symbol value for the binary data available here. So that's this line will configure the two four five US input admitted register, and it will configure all of the other pins, US output and thus this eight bit data that is used for configuring all the bits of a transistor in the microcontroller. So for that, the steps are simple. I'm just putting you through that. For that, I just want to configure the eight bit binary data. And after that, we just want to find the excellent service model data for the binary data provider using this table. And then we just want to load this sort of external data to be able to register.

EMBEDDED C REGISTER BIT MANIPULATION TECHNIQUES PART - 2

This is a condemnation from the previous project, and in this project, we will see two other registers. So the next is the distress vortex. So there are two places for this Botox register. And if they pin this US output, this Botox register is useful for writing zero or one to the particular pin for making this particular pin high or low. And if the penis contouring adults input this Botox register is used for enabling or disabling the internal polyps for the party. Not. And again, this small indicates that this is varying based on the we are contributing and based on reports we have could be. Port, see on Port B, so Port B is having a bridge starting from zero to seven and Port sees having seven bridges starting from PCs zero to between six and seven is not available on port, these having a bridge starting from pretty zero to 87. And one in particular will make the particular business high and zero on spin will make it look. If the business confidence input one only particular pin will enable the pull ups for the particular pin and zero on the pin will disable the for the particular pin.

CONTROL REGISTERS FOR GPIO

PORTx➔8bit register used to write or read the state of the pin(High/Low).

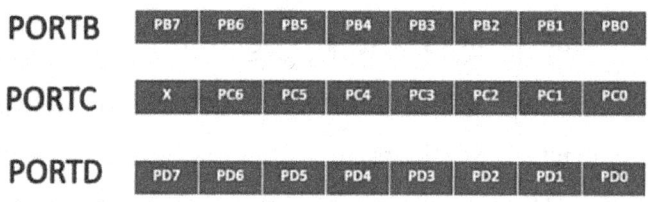

Let's dig deeper. Consider that all these points are configured as output so we can make all these points high or low using this portability. So you're quite right the value one to a particular bitcoin import is the stuff that will be high on these things. I think we don't know that particular bit that will be low, but that's all about the logic on. Let's take an example to understand this. That is, if I want to turn on this output and be zero, I can just drive one to it, as we saw before. That can be done by looking at individual bits of metal, right? That is, I am right. But be auto equal to one left. Some tough be visible. As we saw in the video conference, in part, we can also say it has been using the slime, but this line will certainly be a little bit of poetry. And if they want to turn off this output, be zero, I can write or be Amberson equal to nuggets and all one left to be visible. So this line will clearly be zero, irrespective of its position on this line will certainly be zero, but irrespective of the value that it's holding.

CONTROL REGISTERS FOR GPIO

PORTx → 8bit register used to write or read the state of the pin(High/Low).

1 – HIGH
0 – LOW

PORTB	PB7	PB6	PB5	PB4	PB3	PB2	PB1	PB0

if I want to turn ON this output pin PB0

PORTB |= (1 << PB0) ;

if I want to turn OFF this output pin PB0

PORTB &= (~(1 << PB0)) ;

And let's take another example: if I want to turn on the baby seven six five four Prince, I can write that eight bit binary data to the sport to be registered as we did for d b r extra that I can write zero x for starting this war, which I just want to. You want to work on clearing this for prints. I just want to give zero to it so I can write one one one one zero zero zero zero. So then, after loading the eight bit binary data to the register, I can convert this eight bit between two equal amounts of data. So this method is nothing but the eight bits method that we signed that babies are equidistant right. So splitting these efforts into order must be unfair. And that's so. The R must be one one one one on the list. B is zero zero zero zero, so the equal and hexadecimal value for these two was yeah and zero, as you can see in this table. So the XOR value for Port B is zero zero. I can write this X value to the Sport B for setting these four bits from four to seven and four, creating P zero to be B three.

CONTROL REGISTERS FOR GPIO

PORTx → 8bit register used to write or read the state of the pin(High/Low).

1 – HIGH
0 – LOW

PORTB	PB7	PB6	PB5	PB4	PB3	PB2	PB1	PB0

if I want to turn ON the PB0,PB1,PB2,PB3 pins

PORTB = 0x11110000
MSB   LSB
PORTB = 0x 1111 0000

PORTB = 0xF0

And if the business is configured as input, this port tax register is useful for enabling or disabling the collapse of the PIN. So all the DPA opens in our microcontroller are having internal pull ups in this country. US input This product is useful for enabling or disabling the pull ups of the PIN. You can do for any print using the Port Beatport C and Port Distance, but if this were to be sent, the pull ups will be enabled and if this bit of cleared pull ups will be disabled. That's all about the logic on the next to the Distress Index register. If the corresponding buttons configure the input and be the Cortex register, you can read the status of the PIN using this PIN next register and once again, this small x indicating that this is not a constant and devalues weighting depending on the registrant that we are reading, that we have opened against us Pinap in C and Bwindi. And if we want to leave the status of the pin zero, I can write the condition for performing that, that is pin b Amberson. No one left the BBC that this will be zero. I will execute this condition or I will execute this condition if the corresponding between the DV are OK, but this stuff is considered input. You can read the status of the PIN using this pin next resistor and once again, the smallest indicating that this is not a constant and the values vary. And we have four different registers that have been in between C and PIN B. So let's take an example, if I want to read the status of the bin being zero in being beaten after I can write the condition for performing that, that if you've been beaten, I'm better. No one left the door open, zero. I will execute these lines. If this is false, I will execute this length. So let's understand this. Let's assume the pin because initially zero zero zero zero zero zero zero zero, if the penis configured as input in a microcontroller that can be in varying states depending on the external sources, such as buttons, the control of that pin cannot be controlled by the microcontroller, right? And the next. The statement that this one left at the top end is zero, but gives the input data value zero zero zero zero zero zero zero one. And whenever we configure up enough input, the control of that pin cannot be accessed by the microcontroller, right that will be accessed by the external device, suggests Button. So whenever that corresponding pin, let's take the same thing that has been visible.

CONTROL REGISTERS FOR GPIO

PINx → 8bit register used for reading the status of the input pin.

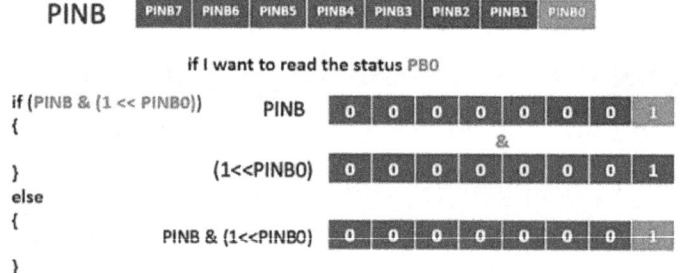

```
if (PINB & (1 << PINB0))
{

}
else
{

}
```

Whenever that corresponding pin value is low, you can see when we perform an operation of these two values. This pin p value will be remaining in the low speed. So we know that the state of that Twitter button is giving low to the microcontroller that will be remaining in the low state and the pin. We will be having the values 0000-00-00. So Amberson of these two values will give us zero after the lesson. So this condition will be filed under this, but will be executed whenever the Swift does, giving a positive input to the microcontroller. This B value will become high. And now you can see an operation of these two bits will end the value one. And that is something the one is nothing but true. So this connection will be executed and this year's content will be neglected. But this is how you think. Pen register. You can read the status of the corresponding pin when it is configured as input. Conclusion for configuring the winner's input or output, BD Orix registered monarchs can be B-BBEE R, B, B, R C and D B R B, depending on what you are configuring. This for study is useful for setting or clearing be particular, but when the corresponding consists configured as output. Under this, you'll support enabling or disabling the plot of the pin. Wendy in this country, the input this small looks can be also for people to see and Port B on this pin next to the step it's using for reading the status of the input pin. This is useful for only one purpose if the pin is configured as input. You can read the status of the PIN using this pin register on this monarchs can be in C and pin b, depending on the input you are reading.

INTERFACING LED WITH ARDUINO

We are just going to build our first and basic project off a little link in our order, no development, but using the registered level programming. So we know that we have an onboard energy available in our order on board on this alibi with the name connected to the digital twin 13 of our panel coming back to our P.A.. You can see that developing 13 is going to be five of our three to eight microcontrollers. And we are just going to put a beat on the bin and we are going to topple the state of the spin for every one second. So going to our order, no I.D. and Nancy, I said we're just going to write the programming lanes for configuration in this wide setup, and we're just going to implement our logic in the white blue. So in the previous work on Figueres and Project, we just learned how we can set on clear bits of paper trying to innovate even on microcontrollers. And we saw some of the logic related to that. And in this project, we are just going to use some of the logic that we saw in that project. So I would suggest you go back to that project if you have not seen it and then come back to this project for better understanding. And initially, as I said, we just want to make this file as output or we can see. We just want to configure this B-BBEE file as output that can be done by writing one to BBB, five bits of b r be registered.

```
void setup()
{
    DDRB |= (1<<DDB5); // PB5 = O/P
}

void loop()
{
    PORTB |= (1<<PB5); // PB5 = HIGH
    delay(1000);
    PORTB &= ~(1<<PB5); // PB5 = LOW
    delay(1000);
}
```

```
Global variables use 9 bytes (0%) of dynamic memory, leaving 2039 bytes for local variables. Maximum is 2048 bytes.
Invalid library found in C:\Program Files (x86)\Arduino\libraries\Keypad: C:\Program Files (x86)\Arduino\libraries\Ke
Invalid library found in C:\Program Files (x86)\Arduino\libraries\Keypad: C:\Program Files (x86)\Arduino\libraries\Ke
```

So I can write B D R B are equal to. One lips of tough. Baby, be fine. So this will configure the. BP, U.S. output. That's all about the configuration, but coming toward logic inside the infinite loop. Initially, I just want to turn on B, B, B five and so that can be done by setting or giving a value one to be B fuel or B register so I can write code B or equal to one laps of golf bb file. And this will make me.

Before I ask how you are. And after that, I just want to wait for one second, and I am going to use the delay that is available in this order, no iby or does nothing but delay of. Chosen. So this delay function is the second delay, Ponton unquote, producing a delay of one second. I just want to give a value of those on to it as we know those in milliseconds are equal to one second. After one second, we just want to clear B BB five in the Port B so that can be done by Port B Amberson equal to making gifts and off one look of tough b b final. So this will. Maybe baby favors are low. And then again, after that, I just want to wait for one second. So that's all about the logic you can see I'm making the baby favors high and I'm waiting for one second. So deep five will be five for one second. And that's one second. I'm clearing the baby and I'm making it slow and I'm waiting for one second when the baby favors low after that one second. This process continues as these four lines are available in the infinite loop of the program. So the only character to be before you make three to eight are Digital Pen 13 of Ordinal will blink at a rate of one second. I know the programming is complete. I don't know how to build this program or to make it compelling. Click on this icon. You can see the campaigning is done. No Canada order, no ball to your PC, USB-C port, no USB cable and and connecting that, click on this aronberg icon for uploading the code to the what are the No. No, I'm applauding the program to the ordinary. You can see the code has been successfully uploaded to what Padrino microcontroller? And the entity that is going to be developing 13 of order, no or be five of US military to aid, it's blinking at a rate of one second.

7 SEGMENT DISPLAY WORKING EXPLAINED

In this project, let us try to understand the working principle of seven segment displays. So these seven segment displays are most commonly used in rating scale DVD players. What does stop clock speed on weakness, etc.? Almost in all applications, vast numbers need to be displayed. These seven segments display audio. So basically, this seven segment displays on nothing but eight. It is arranged in this fashion such that they can display numbers from zero to nine. So as I said, these are the abilities. This is a b, c d e, yeah, Andy. And this dot to pitch and the terminal for this is abcdefg on it. This is the common dominant. As I said, these are alibis based on dominance of Lily, these seven segment displays are classified into two types. We know that a lady has A. and got so in subsequent displays. Out of Pluto's common cathode, uncommon a.m., Let's try to understand. These two types of display. First, we will take it. Common capital display.

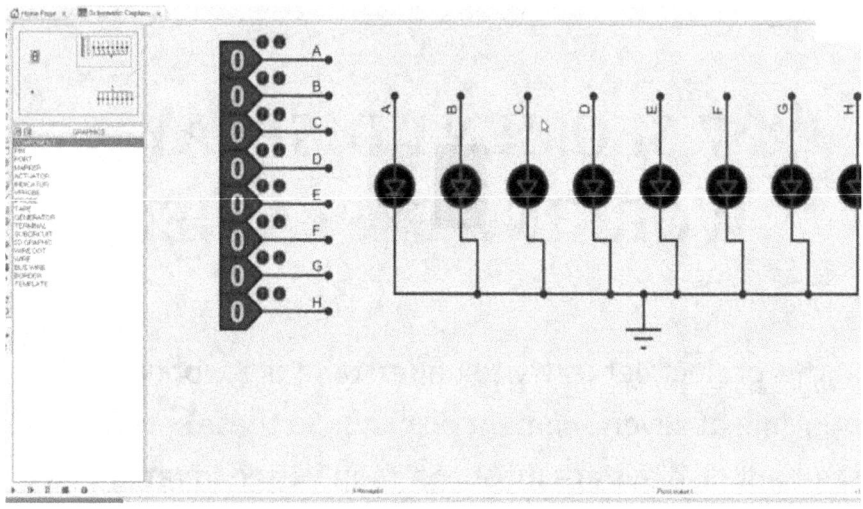

So let's assume that these are the eight that are available in this segment, and this is the A B C, D E F D and this lady and according to that arrangement. So physically this seven segment will look like this. And this centerpiece are the common points which are internally sorted through the sentence. We must provide a common supply based on the type of display, so this is a common cathode display, so you can see, as the name says, all the cathodes of al-Libi are commonly sorted and provide that ground. So this is the common terminal. So in the case of a common cathode, we must provide ground to the common man and, I hope, counter logic to the suppressed thermal anodes of it. And it is. When it's turned on this eight minutes simply wants to say this and it gets lit up. Similarly, B C B e if the road hits so whenever I supply a busted supply for the anode of the common cathode display they respect, it will be like a rock. So this is the working principle of common cathode and the internal structure of common cathode sub segment display. Nonviable kbe. Now we will see the common A. display. These are the illnesses of common display, as the name sees all the energy of the scientific display, ladies are connected commonly and given a common terminal, and we will play a positive role to the common Britain and the capitals of Italy's left free. That is a b c d e f t hat. So I hope the logical probe that and. When they supply a ground to the state by providing a loaded zero, this gets loaded up. And similarly, BCB if Z and Hits will be lighted up whenever a supplier goes down to the respective terminal bids. So this is something that is the working principle of common A. display. And no, let's try to understand.

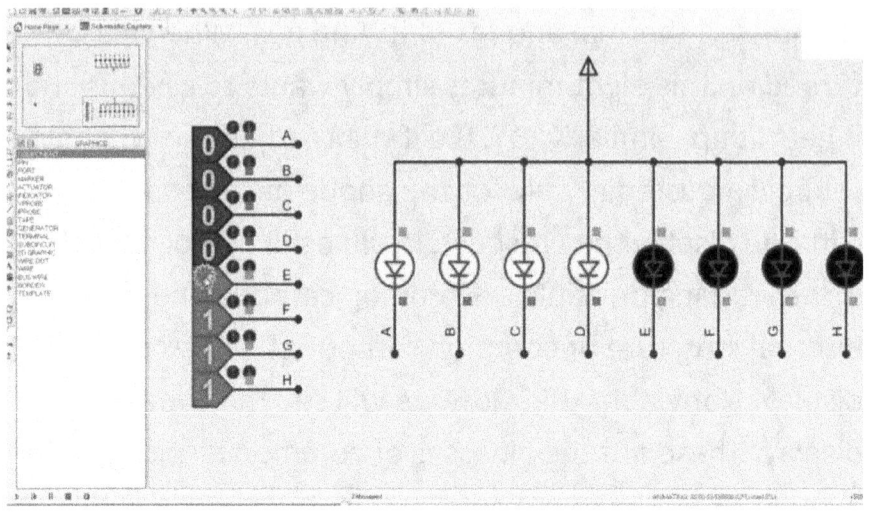

This seven segment display and Olympics pixel values for the sub segment display are now. We will try to understand the seven segment display simulation and how we can derive the Acropolis. What zero to nine. So the display that you're seeing here is common gothard display. So I have I have connected the ground to common pin and this is the pin that I have connected to the zero, the bit of the microcontroller. The microcontroller can be anything, any microcontroller that you are using and this is to meat that is going to one three two three four. To Saudi. This is the IT terminal that is going to triple zero to bits of any microcontroller. So this is a common cathode display, and I have connected the common pin of the display to grant. And now I hope I'm going to think all the eight bits of seven segment display to eight bit microcontroller, but not this year to zero to be for us to see. The second would be to treat it before the proof of the day to 260, but I'm here to seventh. So in this fashion, we are connecting it to the motor controller. Now let's try to drive the is four zero two nine. So for displaying. No zero. I just want to turn on the. Five, four three two one one zero. But this year, B C E. So the exact value for displaying the number zero is zero zero one one two three and one one one one is yeah, zero three of their displays, zero in this common cardboard display. And if I want to display number one. The exact values zero zero six and if we want to display number two. I just want to give an example, your 06 5B. If I want to display number three. The Excel values zero exporter, if I want to display no for. Zero, six, six. Five, zero, six feet. Six. 0X, 7c or 0x. So Wendy can use both for sex and for displaying summon. Zero, zero seven. Eight. Is seven. Man, zero six. Six of. So these are the extra four numbers from zero to name in common cathode display zero one two three four five, six seven, eight and nine. Now, let's see. Common A. Display. As we know, common pins of the common and or display must be gathered to be real and in the similar fashion as we did for the common cathode. I hope to connect the terminal from ear to B2 zero two seven Typekit of any microcontroller. No, initially I will turn all the bits.

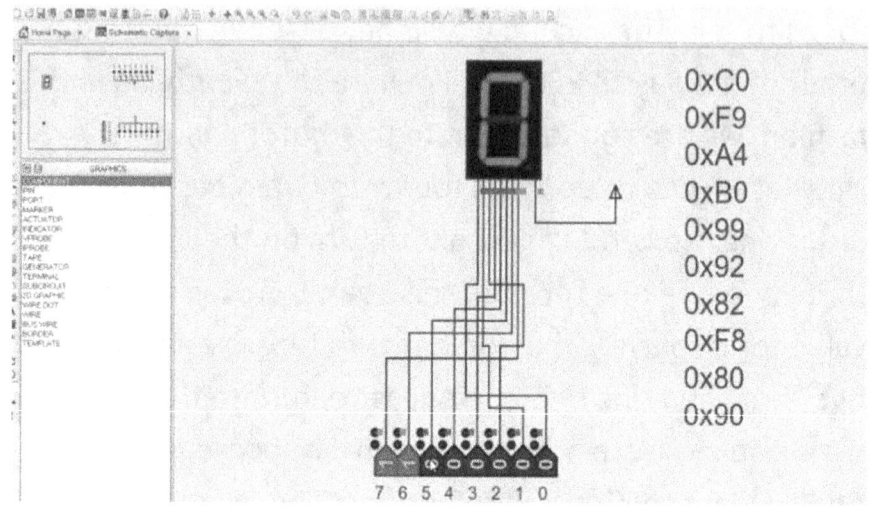

As we know, if you don't own the bits in common and all the bits will be torn off. So for displaying zero. I just want to provide some value Xerox seasonal for displaying, not one, for displaying one. I just want to provide an extra value 06 if nine. For displaying number two. I just want to give an example, your Xerox effort. For three weeks, our values. Zero zero one four four. Zero six nine nine five zero six nine two one four six. Zero, six, eight, two, four seven. 0X if eight. An eight. Zero six eight zero four nine zero six nine zero. So these are the exact values for. Numbers zero, two men in common A. Display zero one two three four five, six, seven, eight and nine. So now we have believed the example is four numbers from zero to nine in both Common Cathode and Common A. seven segment displays. So in the upcoming project, we will try to interface these seven segment displays to put off a microcontroller for displaying numbers from zero to nine.

INTERFACING 7 SEGMENT DISPLAY WITH ARDUINO

In this project, we are just going to discuss how we can interface someone's segment display to our audience for displaying numbers from zero to nine using registered level programming in our business. Let's get started. So in the last project we discussed the working principle of a seven segment display and their internal arrangement. And this is the physical arrangement of a seven segment display, and this seven segment display has eight terminals plus one common terminal. So eight terminals are A, B, C, D, E, D and BP, and these two are the common terminals that are located in the center. And what we will do is we are just going to connect. All these eight bins today would be off at three to eight with 221 resistors for each pin. That is, I will connect it to pretty zero B to PD one C to PD, to B to really three e to four. And you have to be five D to be D six and B B to B D seven. And for each and every pin, I will be giving up on the one resistor between the terminal and B seven segment. And we will be connecting either this common pin on this common pin to the ground of Arduino. So you can see that PD zero is nothing but digital pin zero PD one one three two with two three three before us four and PD five is five six six and PD seven is digital pin seven. So I will be connecting the seven segment to the order, or from digital pin zero to digital pin seven and the common pin on the seven segment, I will be connecting it to the ground of the ordinal. So this is the physical connection that we want to make. And regarding the programming part, initially, I just want to make all the port pins of what B as output so that can be done by writing 0x to the register, be the odd, be registered right.

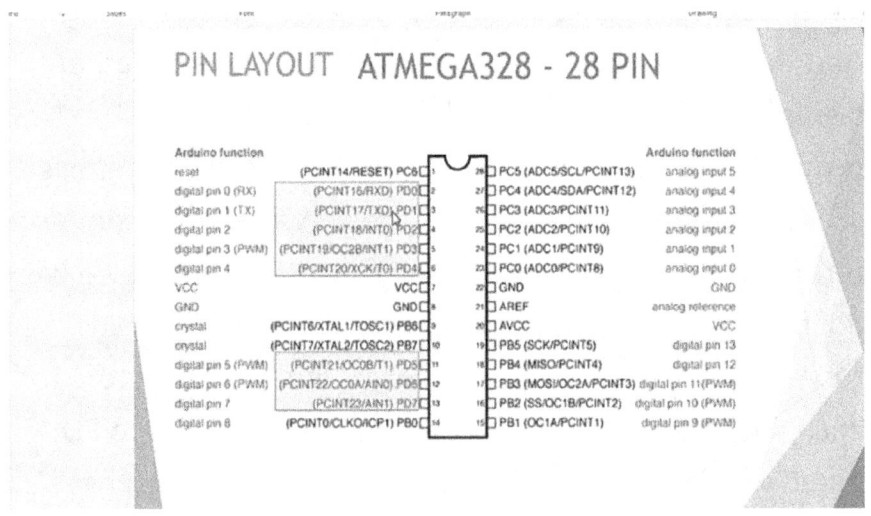

So going into the programming part? I will make all the ports, the princess output. So this will make all the port pins of the port be output. And after that, our programming logic is also simple. And after that, coming to our programming logic, you can see. I'm just going to display numbers from zero to nine in this seven segment display with an interval of one second for each number. So in the last project, the seven segment working project, we just derived some of the highest values for numbers from zero to nine for common cathode uncommon and or display. And I hope you remember this. This is the hexavalent one number from 0.9 on common cathode display. So I'm just going to introduce a common cathode seven segment display to my adrenal. So I will take all these extra numbers from zero to nine, and I will sort that onto the one I renamed. So one segment. So now you can see. So one segment of zero is having the value zero extra three and seven segments of one is having the value zero zero, six and seven segments of two is having the value Xerox vibe. And similarly, all the corresponding numbers are stored in the respective array element numbers. If you want no zero to be printed on this, I wouldn't take my display. I can give the value of. Seven segments. Zero to report. So assigning this value will print be number zero on this, I want to take one display. So if you want no way, I can do seven segments of five. And if we want no nation, I can do something with the name value to the body.

```
void setup()
{
  DDRD = 0xFF;   //PORTD ALL PINS AS O/P
}
unsigned char _7SEGMNT[10]={0x3F,0x06,0x5B,0x4F,0x66,0x6D,0x7C,0x07,0x7F,0x6F};
void loop()
{

}
```

```
PORTD = _7SEGEMENT[9];
_7SEGMENT[0]= 0x3F
_7SEGMENT[1]= 0x06
_7SEGMENT[2]= 0x5B
_7SEGMENT[3]= 0x4F
_7SEGMENT[4]= 0x66
_7SEGMENT[5]= 0x6D
_7SEGMENT[6]= 0x7C
_7SEGMENT[7]= 0x07
_7SEGMENT[8]= 0x7F
_7SEGMENT[9]= 0x6F
```

So in this manner, I have stored the exact values of numbers on the in an addendum renamed seven segments. So in this manner, I have stored the surveillance of numbers from zero to nine on the other named sum and segment. So what they will do is inside the blue. I will invite another loop, which runs from zero to nine. So this loop will start from zero and it will run, it'll be no mayhem, and after Nyom, it will again start from zero and it continues. And inside that, what I will do is I will assign the body value to be. Seven segments of. I. So I'm declaring the variable over here. And under this, I'm giving you. They'll. Thousand men in second. That is one second. So now you can see initially the irony will be zero. And it will take for the Coalition zero less than 10. Yes, it is true. Zero is less than 10. So the control comes inside the loop and the body will be assigned with the value seven segment of zero. So the value zero three will be assigned to be printing the number zero on this seven segment display, and it will wait for one second. After that, I really will be incremental to one. And again, the condition is that this one less than 10 taken and the condition is true. So this could be sustained with the value seven segment of one, which is nothing but zero zero six. And now the number one will be printed on the common cathode, someone's pigment display and after once again, the Ivany will be two. And again, the condition of two is less than 10, which is true. And again, no, this will be attained with the value of any segment of two, which is nothing but zero x 5b. So now the number two will be printed. Similarly, all the numbers will be printed. It will be zero x six. And now you can see after this number, my name is printed. The évolue will be incremental to 10. And no, the condition is endless, then bent with just falseness. So the look will be exciting. And after that, you can see this lupus available in the wide loop, which is an infinite loop. So this loop will run again, printing numbers from zero to nine. And this process continues, and this one segment will be printing numbers from zero to nine until the microcontrollers stop. So that is all about the program. Now I'm building the code using the icon over here. Sorry. I have made a mistake. Now I'm building the project again. I just made a spelling mistake over here.

That was the problem. I know I'm connecting the ordinal to the USB-C port of my PC. And after that, click on this icon for uploading the code to you. What is the number? You can see the program is successful in order to be on the board and for demonstrating the output in the hardware. You just want to build the circuit board that this I'm connecting the Terminal L7 seven segment to digital pin zero of ordinal and Terminal B's contact to digital pin one and see it's counter to digital pin to be connected to digital twin three year contract to the development for Yes office contract to develop and file. And these contractors Digital Forensics and DP are counter to digital in seven of the ordinals and the commentary in 1976, when display you can connect to the ground of audio. And once they start to do better, we can power up the ordinary using an external pole one adapter or using a USB port of the PC, and you can see the output.

16X2 LIQUID CRYSTAL DISPLAY WORKING EXPLAINED

We are just going to see the working of this. The seven segment display can only display numbers, but for displaying characters and alphabets, we cannot use this seven segment as this arrangement cannot fulfill this purpose. So for this purpose, we are going to use LCD displays. They are available in many variants, but display which we are going to use this 16 across to the LCD display. As the name says, there are 16 columns and doodles in this display. Each display element can display one character or no? So totally, we can display 32 characters at a time in this display as we held 16 columns and two rows. Now, let us understand how this display element displays numbers as characters. These display elements are nothing but a fire cross, a dot matrix display, which again has five columns and a truce. Let's see if I want to print the character art in this display. I can make the corresponding bits of the Dot matrix display to be high for doing this purpose. Similarly, can you display any numbers or characters using this dot matrix display? This seems to be very complex, right? Don't worry.

ADDRESS OF DISPLAY ELEMENTS IN LCD

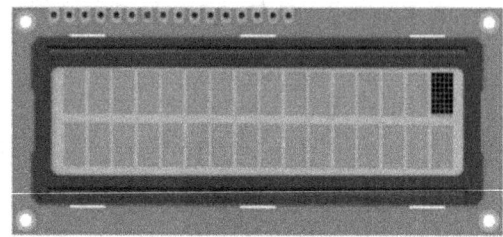

We need not turn on and off each and every bit of dot matrix as every LCD display is coming along with the controller for doing this purpose. Most commonly used controllers are 447 in Zettl from Hitachi. And now this controller has two registers, one in six and one register. Another one is the data register. We just need to do two things. Pass the address at which we are going to print in the in6 and register the data that we are going to print in the data register, then the character gets printed. Address of display elements in a CD starts from zero six eight zero eight one eight two eight three eight four eight five eight six eight seven eight eight nine eight eight b. Eight C A B, eight e eight, if Secondo starts from zero six six zero T one C two three three four three five three six six seven C eight C nine S., A., C., B., C., S., S. B, C, e and see if. You can either pass it with data or forbid data to this LCD.

Here are some of the comments from LCD. Note it down for future reference notes of LCD art. First business we assess with the stick ground paint. Second business really, with just five. Terpenes, which is used for beer in the context of display elements. For business out of that is Ready Select, which is useful for passing the attack to either instruction register. If it is zero, data will be passed to data registered. If it is one that will be passed to instruct and register. And the fifth happiness RW with just the right, which is useful for selecting whether we are just going to read from the LCD or we are going to write to the LCD if audibly is equal to zero right comparison is performed in the LCD. And if equal to one read operation is performed and the next penis enablement, which is the clock enable pin of the LCD, either for reading or writing, we just want to enable this bit. And next to eight bits are B zero, two seven, which are the data lines of the LAPD. Through which we will pass the data to the LCD and the next business and all of the backlight of LCD and next one scatter of the backlight of LCD. And this is the setup for interfacing this LCD to a microcontroller. At first, we just need to define the length of data, or a bit of orbit. And then we will pass the address at which we are printing to the inflection resistor. And then we will pass the data to the data register and the character gets printed. In the next project, we will interface this LCD to a microcontroller.

INTERFACING 16X2 LCD WITH ARDUINO

In this project, we are just going to interface 16 across two LCD displays over ordering or both using state level programming. Let's get started. So we know that this is the cabinet of our misattributed microcontroller that is available in the order board. And we are just going to connect directly to this microcontroller in this way. So we just discussed the working principle of the LCD in the previous project, we just discussed some of the addresses of LCD and also a body with notes of the LCD. And we are just going to connect the data lines all the eight today or be of a lot of microcontroller letters. I'm just going to collect data nine zero two zero. And we you want to be one really want me to be read to be three to three before Betty Ford be five to be defined by six to six and be seven to seven. And after that, we just want to ask R.W. unable to be B B zero, b b one and B two of or B of a one microcontroller. So that's all about the connections. And regarding BBB and IEEE, we will see that in the later portion of this project. And one more thing that you want to remember is that while programming at the register level in your order, no, we will be considering one or two pin numbers. And while you are making the physical circuit connection, you know one ordering a vote. You just want to see this business that is highlighted in red that the data lines of LCD will be counter to digital point zero to digital pin seven and the artist is an enabler of the LCD will be connected to digital pin, a digital pin name and digital content.

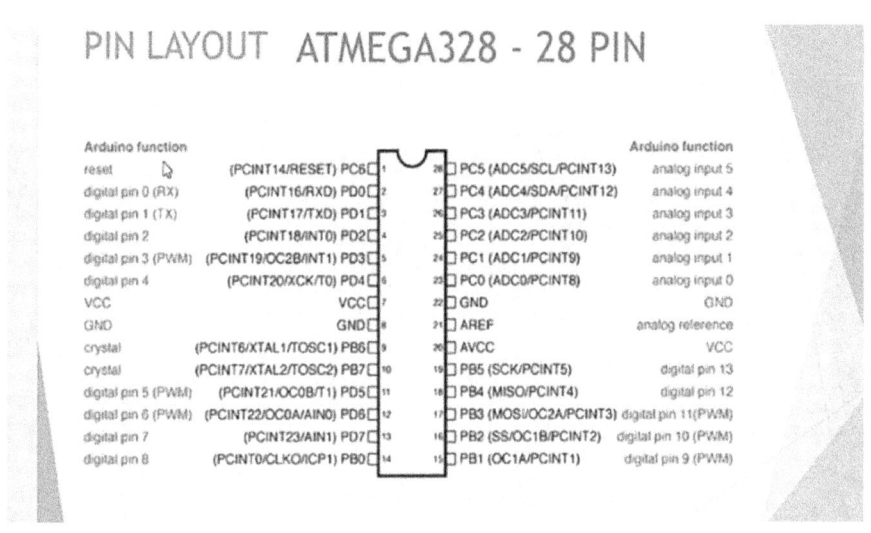

And once connected, initially, what we want to do is we just want to make all these points that the sport be all the pins on board, be zero, b b one and B B to us output or we just want to conquer all these princess output. So coming to our program. This line will configure all the pension pot beats as output. And I just want to conquer the P zero, p one and B to also s output that can be done by writing. So this will configure all the artists RW and enable prints of the LCD also as output. So I have gone to get all the pins of the microcontroller that is connected to the LCD output. Now we will see the programming function that needs to be written for interfacing this entity. I have written four different programming content that needs to be defined for interfacing this entity, that feedback must.

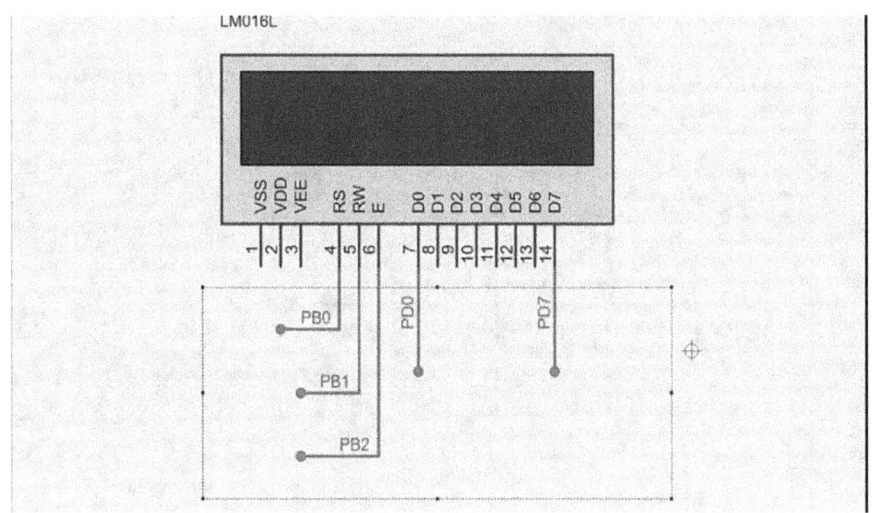

So the first function is LCD data consent, so this function is also for writing data to the LCD data that needs to be printed to the entity. So as we know from the previous project, this function is used for writing to the data registry of the LCD. And it presents a parameter in the name of variable data. So the first thing that we will do is we will pass the data that we receive to this function. So the data lines of the incident, as we know the Netherlands, are connected to the body. So I'm passing the data to the. Or. And secondly, for passing the data to the data registry of LCD, we just want to be honest with you, we want to write this we saw in the last project. And after that, we just want to make the RW bit as zero for writing to the city. And then we are enabling the clerk of the city by setting the enable pin of the LCD and we are waiting for a small delay of 10 millisecond. And after that 10 minutes, we're. Clearing the enable bit of empty. So this is the sequence for writing for the data with this stuff. And this is the function for writing the letter to the entity. And the second function is entity command. This function is used for writing to the instead of sending the self entity that this episode used to force a man to become an entity. This also uses the same procedure as data consent, but it is also receiving a parameter in a variable name called the command and coming into the function.

```
void lcd_data(unsigned char data)
{
    PORTD = data;
    PORTB |= (1<<PB0);      // RS=1
    PORTB &= (~(1<<PB1));   // RW=0
    PORTB |= (1<<PB2);      // EN=1
    _delay_ms(10);          // 10mS
    PORTB &= (~(1<<PB2));   // EN=0
}
void lcd_cmd(unsigned char command)
{
    PORTD = command;
    PORTB &= (~(1<<PB0));
    PORTB &= (~(1<<PB1));
    PORTB |= (1<<PB2);
    _delay_ms(10);
    PORTB &= (~(1<<PB2));
}
void lcd_string(const unsigned char *str,unsigned char length)
{
    char i=0;
    for(i=0;i<length;i++)
    {
        lcd_data(str[i]);
    }
}
void lcd_initialise()
{
    lcd_cmd(0x38);
    lcd_cmd(0x06);
    lcd_cmd(0x0C);
    lcd_cmd(0x01);
}
```

Initially, we will be forcing the parameter of this function into the data lines of the entity. So we know that the Italians or de Silva are passing the command to the UN, for passing the data that we receive. So the instructions with the stroke inside, we just want to clear the oddest bit of entity. And after that, we will make the audibly bitter zero for writing to the NCD. After that, we just want to enable the clock of the basic thing we enable. And then after that, we just want to give us more delay. The result in milliseconds, once this 10 millisecond is expanding, we will be enabled by nothing else. So this is all about the command function for the city, and it is used for writing to the insects and with the stuff LCD and. This one's interesting also for passing comments to the incident. So this one's going to feel like passing one bit of data to Anthony and this one confusion for passing one bit of instruction intensity. And you can see another function called elicited string. This one is used for passing strings of data to see. As you can see, this one when news of the Sam Franklin LCD attack instead of Lou Ford passing a string of data, let's understand the working of this function. You'll see an example. So I'm calling this string function of. So parameters of honesty, saying that this array of characters, so I'm giving this thing to be in B, C and second parameters meant of this string as I know it, be seeds of lent for, I'm giving full. And you can see when they call this function using these two parameters that this ABCD coming forward, the control comes in, said this function on this loop will be executed that this I will be influenced to zero and it will take for this condition that this zero less than nothing, but for zero less than for this group. So the control comes into this loop. Now you can see a little bit of spraoi.

```
 5        PORTB |= (1<<PB0);      // RS=1
 6        PORTB &= (~(1<<PB1));   // RW = 0
 7        PORTB |= (1<<PB2);      // EN = 1
 8        _delay_ms(10);          // 10mS
 9        PORTB &= (~(1<<PB2));   // EN = 0
10    }
11    void lcd_cmd(unsigned char command)
12    {
13        PORTD = command;
14        PORTB &= (~(1<<PB0));   // RS =0;
15        PORTB &= (~(1<<PB1));   // RW = 0
16        PORTB |= (1<<PB2);      // EN = 1;
17        _delay_ms(10);          // 10mS
18        PORTB &= (~(1<<PB2));   //EN = 0;
19    }
20
21    lcd_string("abcd",4);
22    void lcd_string(const unsigned char *str,unsigned char length)
23    {
24        char i=0;
25        for(i=0;i<length;i++)
26        {
27            lcd_data(str[i]);
28        }
29    }
30    void lcd_initialise()
31    {
32        lcd_cmd(0x38);
33        lcd_cmd(0x06);
34        lcd_cmd(0x0C);
35        lcd_cmd(0x01);
36    }
```

We know that zero zero zero will be printed using LCD data from the spot of zero is nothing, but yeah, so it will be printed once that is. The Ivany will be incremented. That's the one. Again, the lesson will be taken and also one minute less than four. This condition is true. So note the altitude adult instead of one will be present with this nothing but be. Once this has been done again, the evening will be incremental to two. And again, the condition is no more so to was less than what the condition is to elicit in a towel. If we are off to this point that it is nothing but see. One of the things I use intimately to three and now also the condition is that this dream has been done for the sick and it is true now. The altitude itself is of trees, planted with just nothing but be. Now that's all. Elements in the string, this better know the condition of Tikrit after incrementing. Now the rivalry will be fought once it is implemented and now when the condition is strict, you can see all it's them for this fall. So the control exits the slope. So that's the thing that is forbidden and the perimeter of the LCD screen function of sprint data with the help of provided. On the next frontiers, you'll support interlacing the LCD. So these are the four common things that need to be provided for the LCD for students six A. zero six three eight. This is 60 and CD in 16 column format, which is nothing but zero, three eight. And this comment directs 06 and see also what is implementing the curvature of the CD once the current display element of the printer on the LCD? Undeterred, in section zero, they don't see anything but display an uncut set off. And the 14 six zero zero one with just nothing but. So for interlacing the LCD, you just want to provide this for instruction at the beginning. So now I'm copying all these functions, all the four functions and then pasting. A body was set up. Plus, the thing that they don't want to do is I just want to call this LCD Union's Liz Swanson inside the that the. And after that, inside the infinite blue. I'm going to the. First line, first call them off the CD by giving the commands zero eight zero. So I just discussed the address of the LCD in the previous project. If you have any queries regarding the addresses of LCD. Well, back to the project and then come back to this project and I will print this string. Embedded. We just saw Flint eight. And then I will go to the. Second line, first column of the LCD and I will put it into the screen. Systems, which is offline seven.

So that said. The string important will be printed on the first plane of the LCD, and the systems will be printed on the second line of the LCD. So that's all about the program. Now I'm building the project, using the icon over here and compiling it. Saudi. They made a mistake with this. There is no function call command. I have named it CMB. Now I'm building the project. We're going to see the compilation, the successful No Connector Order, No Boat to ABC through USB cable after that, click on this. I don't want Icon to upload the program onto what ordinary? You can see the program is successful because of the microcontroller in our robot. Now, will the circular see the output in the hardware? You just want to connect the business to ground needed to power the power supply that is fired, and this we must be counter to a potential murder or variable rates instead of using this variable resistor. You can fine tune what form contrast that is available in newer LCDs.

INPUT DEVICES WORKING LOGICS EXPLAINED

Switches are the simplest form of input devices that can be interfaced with the microcontroller. But for interfacing these devices, we just want to know about two different logics for these input devices. One is pulldown logic and another one is logic. Let's get into deep with these two logics in this video. Unless they don't understand about these things. Let's get started. The first one is, to put it, logic. Here you can see I have connected one end of this switch to the positive rail, another end to the terminal node. This terminal load further goes to the DPA for any microcontroller. And here I just kind of connected a logic pro for analyzing the signal on this double node which is further connected to a register of 10 kms and that goes to the ground. So let's see this simulation of the circuit. I'm turning on the simulation. And initially, when the switch is not pressed, the tumlin node or the deep, the microcontroller is having the logic zero. And when I pressed the switch. The current starts flowing from the Boston Rail to the eye of the metro controller, undetermined notice made height. So when they released the switch. Suddenly, the logic one becomes zero. That is because of this 10km system. That is dispositive rain is certain over here, and the excess current that is available over here will be pulled to the ground through this 10km system. This one is a certain spot when compared to this one for the current available over here. So the current available over here will put more in this direction. And we just got a new trellis over here. So because this 10km sister pulls the current over here to the ground, this resistor is named as pulled on the sister and the logic is named as follows: that is pulled down a lot. You just want to remember that in pulldown logic when the button is released. I walked in microcontrollers having the state zero, and when the button is pressed, the DP a vote will be made height. We will see it next time.

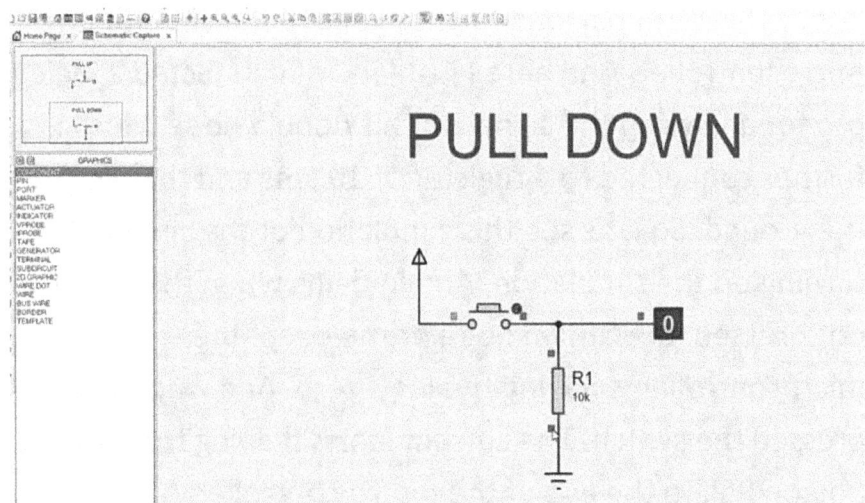

That city will apply here, the case reversed. That is, I hope, connected one end of the button to the ground, another end of the button to the eternal node and the logic probe. And this terminal node is connected to the power rail route and gets us to. And when initially the button is not pressed.This despite this terminal illness, despite this being off of 10km sister and when I press this button. We can't take this part and neutralize this ground. I'm leaving. DP, I want the microphone to lay low, as this is the lowest part for the northwest, part for the current. And this will not flow over here. So we need at least this button, this depth here and move to the DP out of the microcontroller. Got into this here and it will move today. DP, I walk the microcontroller. So pull up logic. You must know that when the button is released, the DPA will be having the high signal and when the batteries press the DPA, what will be having zero signal, which just the reverse of will not. So in the next project, we will try to interface.

INTERFACING PUSHBUTTON WITH ARDUINO

This project, we are just going to see how we can interface input devices such as buttons and with just an Arduino, let's get started. So what we're going to do is we are just going to connect the button to the battery to make our data a digital open. And we already know that we have it on board and indeed that is connected to the Big 12 13 of our B-BBEE five three two eight.

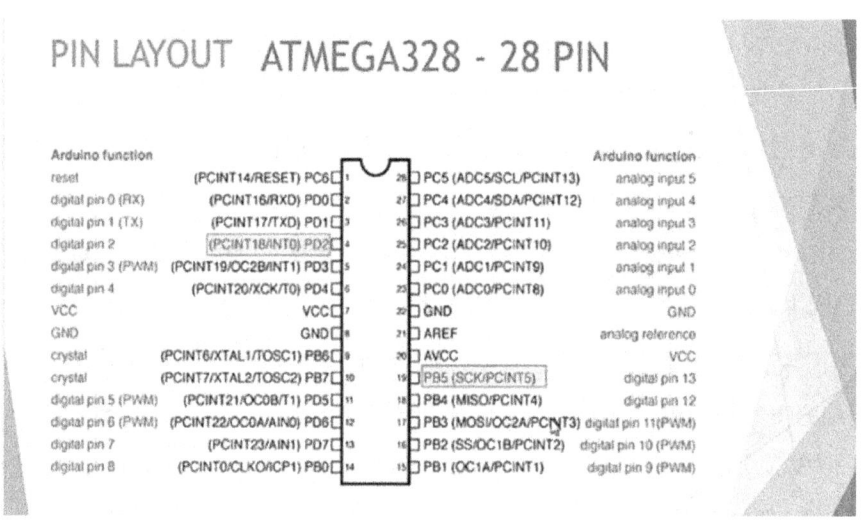

So based on the button status that is guaranteed to really do or do, we are going to vary the state of the country to be developing 13 of our dinner or be five of at three to eight? So in the last input working project, we just discussed the two working principles of input devices that this will do and pull up. So we are just going to implement this pulldown logic. So whenever we press this button character to be nothing microcontroller, Duckpin will receive the high signal. And when we leave the button, we will receive a low signal in the pen, so we will check the status of the PD two billion of the microcontroller. And we know what this means. Hey, that means the button has been pressed, so we will turn on the LCD that is the onboard allele of ordering. That is going to be five four three two eight. And when we release this button, we get a low signal to the microcontroller. So it will be low. So we will turn off the LTE that is available in the order number. Coming to our program, the first thing that we want to do is we just want to configure this baby famous output and this pretty to us input. So this can be done by writing one to a bit of B R B register. So I can write that B R B is equal to one left, so tough b bb fight. So this will configure B, B B famous output. And for configuring this really for us input, I just want to write zero two d b BBB, two bits of baby deregister. So I can write B R B Amberson equal to Magus and one lap of B BB two. So this will configure the period for us. Input. Inside the wide loop, we are just going to implement our logic for this. We are going to take them. Status of this, really to pin an impetus, i.e. we will turn on this baby fight, and if it is low, we will turn off this baby fight. So for that, we are just going to use you to listen in C programming and for taking the input bin status. We are just going to use Britain to be registered. So bin be. But they're not. One lifts off. Bindi, do. If it is true. We will turn on me. Baby fight. Yes. We will turn off baby fights at this port, be Amberson equal to Vegas and all one lapse of a tough TV fight. Coming to our logic, I hope you remember the statement that I explained in this zip: a walk on prejudice and project part two. If you have any queries about how the statement is functioning. Please go back to the letter and then come back to this letter for better understanding. Initially, when departments are pressed, you can see this if conditions are true, and this will make the amity glow, which is guaranteed to be fine, and the listed button means the button that is guaranteed to be read to. And if we release the button that is counter to two of our microcontrollers, this conviction would be false, which will execute the ILS part of the program, which is nothing but it will turn off the al-Libi character to freely fight. It is nothing, but it will turn off the entity that is counter to the baby fight. So we pressed the button, the energy will be lighting up, and if we release the bottle, the energy will be turned off. But that's all about the logic.

```
void setup()
{
  DDRB |= (1<<DDB5); // PB5 = O/P
  DDRD &= ~(1<<DDD2); // PD2 = I/P
}

void loop()
{
  if((PIND&(1<<PIND2))
  {
    PORTB |= (1<<PB5);
  }
  else
  {
    PORTB &= ~(1<<PB5);
  }
}
```

```
Done uploading
Global variables use 9 bytes (0%) of dy
Invalid library found in C:\Program Fil
Invalid library found in C:\Program Fil
```

Now I'm building the code using the icon over here. The builder will now connect to a new development board to show you what we see through the USB port and then click on this Aramark icon for uploading the code to your Partner Development Board. Now the program is successfully bought into a microcontroller, so no, you just want to build a cycle that is going to push the button to the digital pin two of no. And on the other side of the button connector five firewall power supplies on in the same digital pin terminal, pull down using a 10km toaster and on the other side of the 10km system cannot be grown. So that's all about this attitude. And now you can see whenever I press this button, the lady that is available in the Ordinary Development Board that is going to happen 13 will be lighting up. And when Mr. Button, the lady will be turned off. Thanks for reading.

ELECTRO-MECHANICAL RELAY WORKING EXPLAINED

We are just going to see water release and how would this function? Another way that we will see how we can build a circular, which is useful for controlling this release from my deep a warfare microcontroller and this circuitous useful for controlling 230 worlds if the appliances using this release. Let's get started. So what is released and these are nothing but switches or in other words, we can see these are electromagnetic switches that are useful for controlling high powered devices from the low power signals. Let's take one example to understand that. So for controlling the state of a lady, we can directly connect the and all of the injury to the DPA, the microcontroller through some resistor value, and then we can connect the cathode of the elite to the ground of this attitude so that we can control the state of the LCD by using the power delivered from the deep microcontroller. As we know, these images are low power to make this that is consuming less amount of power that is delivered from the microcontroller. But for controlling a 230 world or 110 moles AC light, we cannot actually cannot be so minimal. The light bulb to the deep a wall of the microcontroller, as we know of a microcontroller, will be mostly operating between three point three voltage to rival DC, and this one will blow one leg with the help of 230 volt or one panel AC, which is the power signal than the signal that is delivered from the microcontroller. So here comes the purpose of the relay for controlling the high power devices. So you think they really you can control the 230 world is in lightbulb on this really can be triggered an entree good with this small amount of signal that is delivered from the microcontroller, so forth that we just want to build a simple set to play for controlling the state of Sydney that is for energizing and energizing the goal of, didn't it? So there are varieties of releases available in the market.

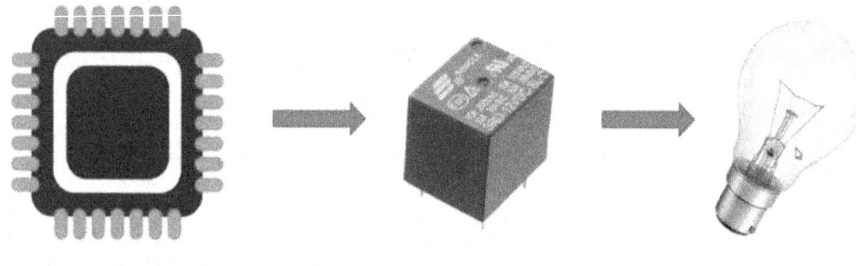

And one of the most commonly used to remember this silver jubilee, and I'm just going to use this really for controlling the state of the world is the light bulb with the help of low power by volt signal. And you can see these relays that were swallowed. And this whole thing is based on the coin voltage rating digitally. So if voters are ordered really, you just want to provide a told roll call of the rally or another thing they call you. So you think there's a firewall, you just want to provide a firewall? I mean, for certain people, literally, we just want to provide the country for all B.S. supply for another cynical rule of tyranny. So based on the coil voltage ratings, there are variants of release available, most commonly used in one spot firewall load and total before release. And you can see this one is the schematic and structure for the Silver Jubilee. And this schematic is common for all the releases, and the working principle is also common for all the releases you need. Don't worry about that. And now you can see these two terminals are dedicated for the call of the release. As I said, I'm just going to use Pololikashvili, so I will be providing all the signals between these two terminals for another day.

Relay Structure

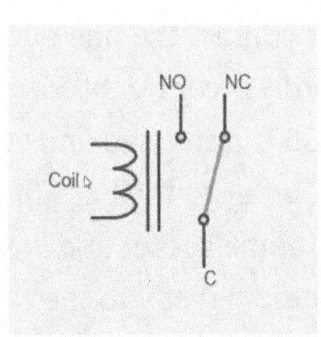 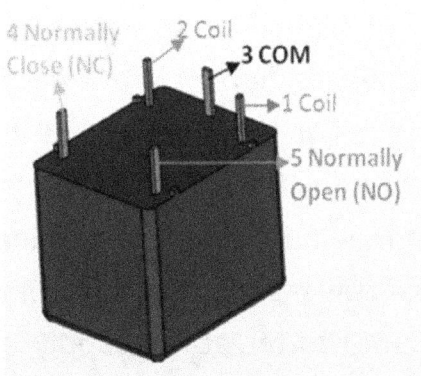

Similarly, this one and two are the coil dominance of the delay. And other than that, we have three different kinds of dominance. See, you know, Anansi, this c is nothing but the common terminal of the delay and this year and sees nothing but the normally closed terminal. So initially, when the delay is not triggered, you can see the connection is made between common and Yancy. And that is why this terminal is named as normally closed on this yennaris nothing but they normally open terminal, and this normally open terminal would be connected to the common terminal. We never did all of the delays anodised, so whenever the coil of the release energized, the common terminal of the delay will be coming in contact with the node terminal, leaving the nted terminal and whenever the coil of the released DRM address with this common terminal will be coming in contact with the terminal, leaving the node terminal. This is the simplest operation of delay, and let's understand this with the help of simulation, and you can see this one as the Tololo. The battery on here negative terminals contact the one end of the call on the other end of the cordless contract today, whilst the terminal through this USB is dismissed and you can see here common terminals counter to the base of the power supply. This is from our home socket and neutral of the power supply is granted directly to the neutral of the light bulb and base of the light connected to the node terminal. And now you can see whenever I press the switch, this will be closed, which will be another coil of this, really. So I'm pressing the switch. You can see this the latest now energized. So the common terminal is coming into contact with the union terminal by just closing this circle so that despite the light bulb over here, it's blowing now. And whenever I risk the sweat, the connection is made between the common terminal and C-terminal, leaving big and not terminal. So this attitude is open now. That is why this light bulb is not doing so. This is the working principle of really whenever the coils and the connection will be made between common terminal and not terminal. And when the coil's DNA dies, contact will be made between the common terminal and the zip terminal. Our next lead, we are just going to discuss about the search tool that helps us to control these myths with the help of the microcontroller. So this is the setup here. You can see this is one of the microcontroller pins. And here I am, connecting the microcontroller to the base of the transistor. We see five four seven through 21 resistors, and the collector of the transistor is counted to be one end of the coil of the delay. On the other end of the coil is contact to the lawsuit. All right. As I said, if you are using a different voltage rating of the delay, so just five alternatives for all, you just want to provide the power supply accordingly and across the coil, I'm providing one nine four zero zero seven diode. And regarding this attitude between, you know, Yantian common, this is the same as we saw earlier in this project. That is, whenever the release is triggered, the common will be coming in contact with the known, closing this support so the light bulb will be blown whenever we see images to be made. The connection will be made between Common and the ANC making this circuit open so the light bulb will not begin. Initially, when providing a zero will signal to the base of the transistor, this plan to start over here will be like an open split that is like this. So this coil will not be energized because this coil terminal is not receiving big ground.

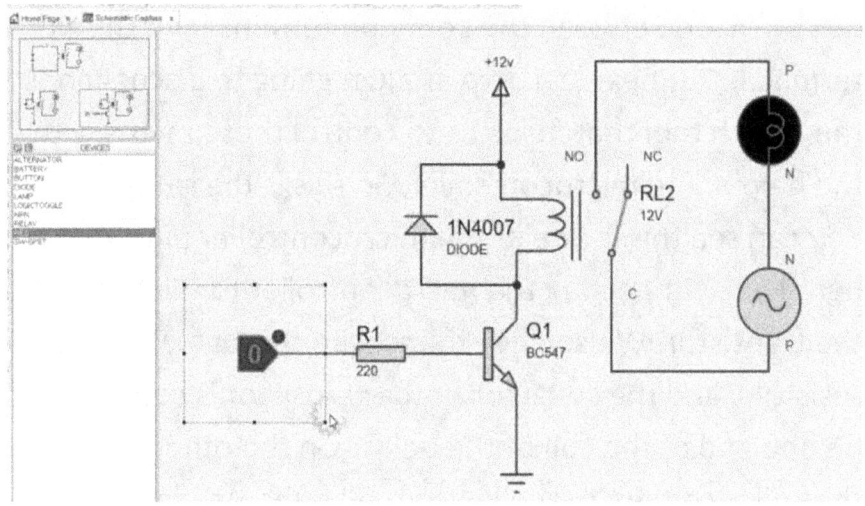

And whenever I provide a high signal to the base of the transistor, the transistor will be acting as close to the switch. So now this coil will be energized because of this circuitous clause and when the coil is energized, the common terminal will be coming in contact with the node terminal. And this light bulb will be blown on, let's say, to demonstrate this now. When I give a zero world signal to the base of the transistor, the common terminal is in contact with the ANC because evil is not anodized. And when they give up, hostile fire will signal to the base of the transistor. We can see the laser energized and the contact has been made between the common terminal and not terminal. So the light bulb over here is doing so. This is the working principle of this cycle. So you can control the state of the really from the award, the microcontroller. So you may be wondering, why do we want this deal? Let's understand that I'm removing the contact between the diodes when they supply a zero will signal to the base of the transistor. The relay will not be adjacent. And Renee, regarding the transistor base, there may be energies now. The current from here will be flowing in this direction and it will be moving through the coil and again it will be neutralized in this ground. So this is the direction of the current. So it will keep on flowing. And when I suddenly supply a zero one signal to the base of the transistor, the current that is available here at that moment will not be having any part to flow. So it will move towards the collector of this transistor at this terminal. So this may need to be damaged by the transistor, and that is why we want this diode. So now, I'm collecting this diet across the coil. Now, if you'll see I'm giving a false tool to the base of the transistor and when they suddenly remove the voltage over here, the excess current that is available over here will have a part in this barracks. And so it will move towards the annual of the diode and it will again flow through this coil so it will move again in this direction. And this process continues until the current is being neutralized. So whenever the current is flowing through this coil, some amount of current is consumed by this coil and this coil will dissipate that current into the form of heat.

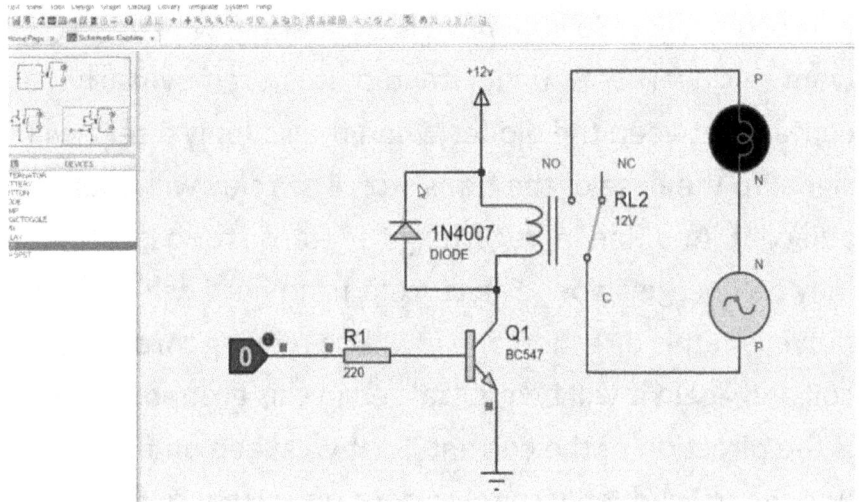

After several hundred times the excess current that is available or stuck up between this terminal will be neutralized because of this diode saving the life of the transistor. That is why this diode is called US feedback diode or free-wheeling diode. You can see I have built the same circuit on a breadboard, and the only change that I made is, I hope, connected a push button to the base of the transistor. So whenever I press the button, a positive firewall signal will be given to the base of the transistor, triggering deadly. So this light bulb, which is available over here, will be lighted up. And when they release the push button, this light bulb will be turned off. So regarding the release circuitry, you can see I have used to the main supply from my socket in my home and you can see the face of play off. My power supply is connected to the common pain of the relay that is over here, and the face of the light bulb is connected to the, you know, pin of the relay that is available over here. And the ANC pin is not connected and the neutral of the light bulb is directly connected to the socket neutral. That's all about this. I don't know. Let's try to demonstrate this slightly when they just push button. The relay will be triggered on this 230 volt Emily light bulb when we light it up and we need at least a button. This will be turned off. I have connected the mains to my socket and I have turned on that. You can see that now when you press this button. You can see the light bulb was turned on on Wednesday, at least important the entities don't owe. So in the next project, we will try to interface this release that you play for controlling 230 World if the light bulb with the help of our microcontroller.

INTERFACING RELAY WITH ARDUINO

This project, we are just going to interface release with the world general, you know, for controlling putative world light up mentis. Let's get started. So I'm planning to build the support for demonstrating the interface, that this is the same, so cute that we built that the relationship was so good that we built in the last project for controlling a light bulb. We also demonstrated the statute. If you have missed that project, you can go back to that project link given in the description and this is the same. So cute. I'm just connecting the base of the transistor to the digital benefit of ordinal and then connecting a push and pull down logic for the digital pin seven ordinal. I'm powering up my ordinal, you know, using the USB-C port of the. And for this, really, I'm using it loudly, so I'm using a well-told adapter for powering up the display.

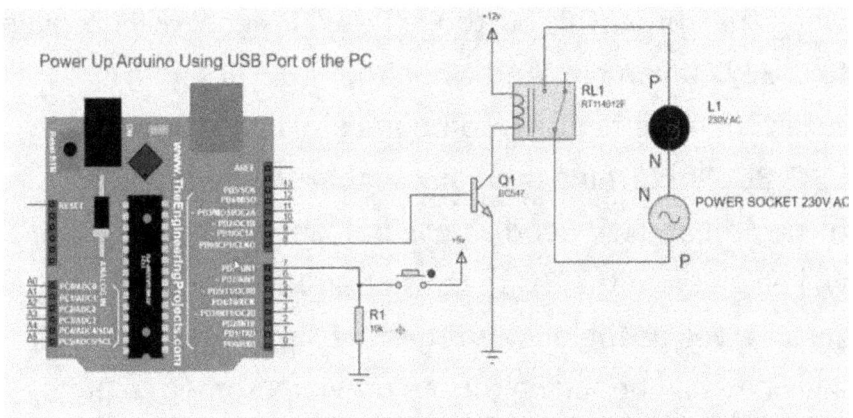

Don't forget to commonly sort the ground up the order nobody knows of the adapter use, reportedly. Let's go to programming. Initially, we just want to configure the pins, right? You can see this pin will be treated as output and this pin will be Manaf input. So this digital pin of or, you know, is nothing but really seven to eight and thus eliminate this nothing but the BP zero three two eight. So I'm making the BP zero US output. So I can be B or equal to one, let's have top BBB zero, so this will configure d b b zero as output mixed fleet. I just want to make the baby seven US input, so I just want to write a zero to that particular bit. So D B R B Amberson is equal to Nagase of one lot of tough b d b seven. This will make me b d seven s input. So they can't go to Goodison Park. They have configured the visitors output and pretty Savannah's input. And regarding the logic, we are just going to turn on this really when nobody was part of it, stressing that when they press this button, a firewall signal will be given to the PD seven pin. And when the firewall signal is received in the beating, someone pin it will turn on the BBC. But I'm turning on really so that the light will be turned on and we need a push button as zero one signal will be given to the BD seven so that I will turn off the PIN zero as well as the dirty word is the light bulb. So for our logic newbie, be taking for the previous someone. If it is high, we will turn on the PD zero. If it is low, we will turn off the BBC. But this year, turning on the 2.0 word, the AC light bulb like this, we are turning on the 230 word light bulb using a really whenever the push button is pressing and we will be turning off the light when nobody push button Islamist so I can take the PD to one by writing the condition will b Amberson off. One lapse of tough. In these seven. So this condition will return one when nobody will be someone with this height that will never be beating someone with this height. So if it is high, we just want to turn it on. There is nothing but BBC Two so I can turn on the TV with zero rating. What is or equal to one looks tough. Be musical. So this will turn on the BBC, though, if the pause button is not president, we just want to turn off the relay right orchestra, be zero. So I will take care of my health.

```
void setup()
{
    DDRB |= (1<<DDB0);   // PB0 = output
    DDRD &= ~(1<<DDD7);  // PD7 = i/p
}

void loop()
{
    if((PIND&(1<<PIND7)))
    {
        PORTB |= (1<<PB0);
    }
    else
    {
        PORTB &= ~(1<<PB0);
    }
}
```

C:\Users\intel\Arduino\arduino-builder -dump-prefs -logger=machine -hardware C:\Users\intel\Arduino\hardware -hard

So whenever the button is president, if conditions will be true, so that whatever they're going to take, if condescension will be executed, that this BP deal relief will be turned on. And whenever we release the button, this condition will be false. So automatically, the condition is false. This ELISpot will execute whatever that is written inside, the export will be executed. Here we have only turned off the people zero so that BP zero will be turned off. That's all about the programming, but now I'm building the code. No, you cannot do it or deny, you know, the development board to the USB port of the PC through USB cable and then click on this icon for uploading this. What is the menu now? The program has been successfully uploaded to you, what are the known, you know, no build a circular to see the output in the hardware. Now you can see I have connected the button for the digital seven or no undeveloped riverside digital of ordinal. And this one is the related website that they built on the breadboard in this project. And here you can see the output in my heart.

INTERRUPTS IN MICROCONTROLLER EXPLAINED

let's discuss what is an interest in a microcontroller and how it looks. As the name implies, interests are used for halting the normal program execution of a microcontroller for executing these set top lines that are available in. Our interests are in. Generally, interests are classified into two types: software interests, hardware interests. Hardware interests are interests that can be provided from the external source to the microcontroller to do what work, task and very good examples of hardware and drops are external and. And software interests are interests that are generated by the inbuilt preference of a microcontroller to perform a specific task. And examples of soccer rental sites, ABC and timer and others are being used. Using interest in a program saves the time for the microcontroller. Let's see how we can save time using the program. For that, we will understand this with an example. Let's take an example of what input program rather a leader needs to be blown when these were just pressed.

INTERRUPTS - EXPLAINED

```
void main()
{
    while(1)
    {
        if(BUTTON == 1)
        {
            LED = 1;
        }
    }
}
```

So this is the main function that we will be writing in almost all the platforms of the microcontrollers. For example, in pilot, because I've been at Akman Studio, but in order not to, this main function will be split into two functions. They are a wide setup and a wide loop, so they are the same main function, but they are split into two different functions. So what are the things that we will be writing inside this main function that is outside this while one they are given instead of a function called why does it? And the things that we are writing about, our tendency to spread wanton cold, wide looks, so why look with nothing but the white one that is available over here? Unwanted setup is nothing but the configuration box that we will be writing outside this white one. But inside the main function. And you can see this is the infinite loop that we are having in every program. And this is the condition for the button. And if the button is high, we will make the elderly feel high. And upset about the program, I have not written any statements for turning it off. If you take a closer look at this program, you can see that if the button is continuously monitored by the processor, irrespective of the status, the button that is in this condition is checked even a bit, so it is not right. So the processor will be always busy doing this process, so it will not have any time for any other process. So it will be continuously monitoring the state of this button using this condition. If it's high, it will turn on the LCD orders. It will keep on taking this condition. So this method is called pulling, but that.

INTERRUPTS - EXPLAINED

```
void main()
  {
     while(1)
        {
        }
  }
ISR()
{
  if(flag == 1)
   {
     LED = 1;
   }
}
```

INTERRUPT METHOD

We will connect button to external interrupt pin of microcontroller

So in this market, you can see the processor will always be busy taking this button step. And let's relay this program using entrapment. So using entrapment, we will take an example of external Interpol. So here also, we will be having a main function. Why remain unanswered that we will be having an infinite loop and we will be having another function called by yourself content that is to interrupt service routine things that I have thought once when we are taking for the flag to be high. This flag does nothing but flag that is allocated for the external interest of our microcontroller. We will be having separate flags for all the inputs in a microcontroller sub par excellence example. The flag will be different for ABC and we will be having another plug. So we will be having different different parts for different, different interests in the microcontroller. So we are taking for the excellent interest flag to be high if it's high. We are making the leap to go. So initially, when the program starts, the microcontroller always starts from the reset button, and after that, it comes to this main function. You can see nothing is happening to the main function, so the control enters into this white one. And it will be saying that as this is an infinite loop and will never be given rising or falling to the external entropy, not the microcontroller, the external peripheral will enter the processor and the processor process all the process that it was doing in the main function inside the white one. And it will come to this IFR function. Coming here, it will take for the current flag to be high and high, it will turn on the enemy or it will execute all the lines that are available in this. And after completing all the lines that are available at once an hour after completing this statement, it will go back to this main function and it will resume the process that is going to pit. So this is the routine for an intern program in any microcontroller, and this interconnection will be called each and every time whenever we give a rising or falling it to the external independent of the microcontroller. So this process is same for all the types of interest, but these sources of interest may vary in case of external interest. The interest will occur when that is a change in external interest in. If you take software in also, the working is the same. But these sources of interest will really, for example, interrupt the process. There will never be a digital canvas and it's completely useless. AARP will interrupt the process whenever you need. Data has been received and will interrupt the process whenever any predefined time has elapsed or expired. I hope you understand what our interests are and how it looks.

IMPLEMENTING EXTERNAL INTERRUPT IN ARDUINO

let me just want to see how we can implement the external program in order using level programming. Let's get started. Initially, we just want to find out the external interruptions that are available in no other. So this is the internal microcontroller. And you can see here this zero ion one are the external instruments that DiSpirito and military are the two external instruments available in Nova 7:57 microcontroller. So this digital two and digital twin three are the two external underpinnings of what Arduino? So what we are going to do is our programming logic is simple.

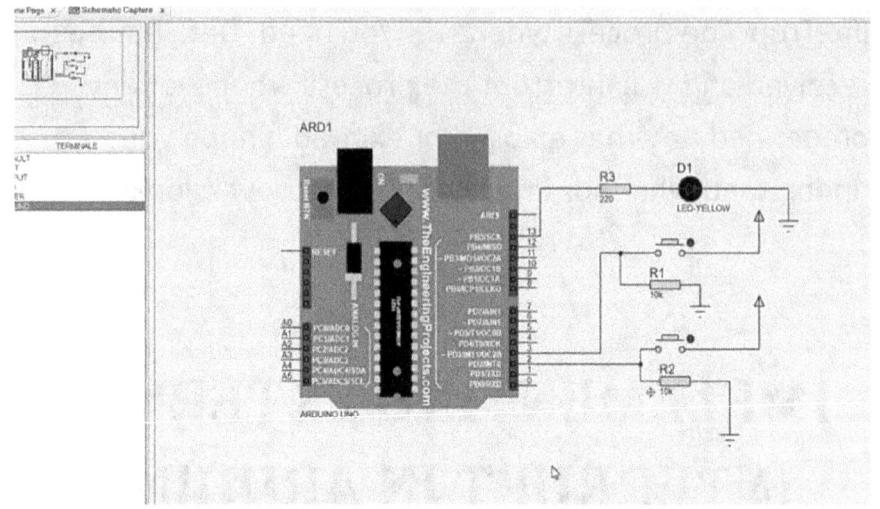

We are just going to connect two buttons to this digital pin two and three in the world's own logic so that whenever I press this button. This developing story will receive a hyperlink, and we may release it. This will receive a low pulse and when we press this button, this development two will receive a signal authorizing it. And whenever I release this button, it will the cevap following it. And we are just going to use the onboard energy that is available in no order, no board as we know we have it. And maybe that is already counter to 13 of the other, which is nothing but be read before you off board. So we are just going to use that. We are not going to connect anything external and maybe for this purpose. So what we will do is whenever I press the button that is connected to IP zero, we will implement a set of codes inside the external entrapping zero Assad. And we will turn on this Ali and whenever I press this button. So regarding the programming logic, what we are going to do is whenever I press this button, this will give a rising edge on the digital pin to that IP zero of the microcontroller. So we will execute a set of lines for turning on this element inside I in p zero. Are you set? So whenever I press this button, we will turn on the elderly. And when they press this button, this contract will be developing three, that this might be one of the microcontrollers. We will see what a set of cords is inside. I shouldn't be one. I just saw what was burning off this allele. So whenever I give it, I think it's the pulse to this developing three that this ain't the one. We will turn off the elderly and whenever we give it, I think it's supposed to be zero. You will turn on the elderly. So for the programming purpose, you're just going to use inter-service, it'll be out of contract and let in our program. So that's all about the logic that we're going to implement. And let's see the steps for implementing this external interference. So these are the steps I am copying and then twisting inside the white circle. So initially, I just want to make this really famous output as we are going to use the Licata to whip it so that can be done by setting the BBB favorite off by the ability to store. So this will make them. We are famous. Output. And after that, coming to our first step, we are just going to enable the global internet enabled alphabet of microcontroller omega three to eight. So for any interest in your program, we just want to set this book. So going to our data set of the eight, if you search for Assad that the state of your status registered, you will get this registered.

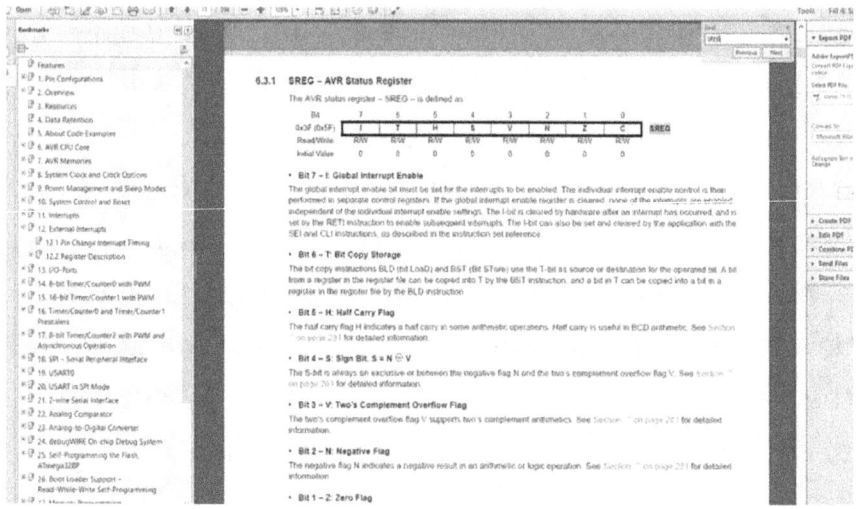

So in this latest study, you can see this seven submitters eye, which is nothing but the global internet enabled big. So for setting the spot, I can write, yes, sorry or equal to one that looks so tough. Seven. So this will set to be a bit of a sad thing that is global and enable it, or you can use an inbuilt function that is provided by the order no I.D., which is nothing but I. So if you call this function, this will also be said to be, I believe, in the authority register. You can either use any one of them at that. I'm using the direct access method on the next step. We just want to enable the required external input from the corresponding register, as I said, as I said, we are just going to use both the Anti Zero and Anti one of our microcontrollers. So we just want to separate these two bits in our external interrupt registers.

```
void setup()
{
    DDRB |= (1<<DDB5);   // PB5 = O/P

    // ENABLE THE GIE (GLOBAL INTTERUPT ENABLE BIT)
    SREG |= (1<<7);
    //sei();
    // ENABLE THE REQUIRED EXTERNAL INTERUPTS FROM THE CORRESPONDING REGISTERS

    // SET THE EDGE SELECT FOR EXTERNAL INTERUPTS

    // IMPLEMENT THE INTERRUPT HANDLER


}

void loop()
{
```

What are the external and under that, click on this register. If you go to the E, you must get registered at the C. External input must register. You can find this ion one ion p zero bits. So these two are the bits that need to be enabled for enabling B identity zero one. So we will set these two bits in the EU register. A musket or equal to one is lots of tough. I'm p zero. Order one lapse of tough I want. So this will enable the external interest zero on the external into one of all microcontroller microcontrollers to eight. And the next step, we just want to sell it to trigger the interest I see. We are just going to give up racing pulse using people's buttons. So we must secure the interest in such a method that whenever we receive that, I think it's on the intercropping, we will generate an interpreter. So you can see we have configured this button in a pull down logic. So whenever we press this button arising, its pulse will be given to entrapment. So we just want to configure this interest in such a way that whenever it arises, its pulse is given to the external and the input, even if it's triggered so fast. Go to the ICRA, register external interest controlled study, and you'll see these two bits. You can set the agenda for ANP one on using these two bits. You can set it to be in default and invisible. They can see if you value zero to these two bits. The low level of MP one then presents an interest request and if they give the value of zero for these, two bits need logic to end on and the one generates an interest request. And if you give a value of one zero to these topics of falling into one generates an interest request. And if I give the value of one one the right thing and I into one generation interpret what's so in our case, we just want to configure these two bits in one one. So I just want to give one of these two bits. I just see one one a nice one zero. And also, we just want to configure one for using zero one nine zero zero. So I went to the Yazidi register. I'm setting them. I see what one zero. Yes, even one. On top of that, I'm setting myself. Yes. Zero zero. ISC 01. So we have configured the rising of its interest request for both the zero and ninety one for a lot of microcontrollers after, but we just want to implement an interest to see. Isaac Hanson. So I am bringing the statement over here. It is interested in all microcontrollers having a separate interest handler. So for I and P zero, the handlers, I just sort of. I have zero underscores. But So this is the interest handler for I.A. zero and four, ANP one. We are the same. One little change we want to make is I know the one underscored by. So this is I guess, our funds and for anyone. And this is the entire panel of title, as I said, little plastic button that is considered to zero. You're just going to turn on the light. And whenever I press this button, which is counter to be one, you're just going to turn off the light. So I am zero. I will set the DPP five, but. So this will certainly be before you make the Olympic glow, but the city is what an idiot, cardinal. In this, I guess, I'm just going to clear the BPP fight. So this will clearly be fine, and it will be on bodily order not to below. So whenever this interest is executed, it will turn on the Navy and whenever this assault is executed, it will turn off the enemy. So let's understand the working of this program initially when the program starts. It will execute all these statements over here in the wide setup, and after that it will enter into this infinite loop. Let us do our loop and it will stay here as this is an infinite loop and we never give up racing its pulse to any one of the Olympic zero or any one and lipstick. Whenever I press this button, the IMT zero will be having a racing trigger and the processor will interfere with the IMT zero vector. So the processor passes all the processes that it was doing here, and it will enter into that function. So instead, this sort of function, we are just turning on the entity so it will make the onboard allele of order known to be high. And after executing all the lines over here, it will go back to the wide loop and it will simply process it here. And whenever we press this button. Which is considered to be one the same process happens, except that they process the process all the process over here, and it will enter into this identity one way to your satisfaction. And here it will exclude all the statements yet that this and I think what it will turn off, the allele that is available on the order. No, not to execute all the lines over here. It will go back to the wide loop and it will resume the process here. So this is the routine of the entire program. So this routine is common for all the programs. But the sources of interest may really since this is an external and we are connecting a button for triggering the interest in case of any other inputs like timer, wasabi or any other interest these sources may be. But the routine of the program is common.

```
void loop()
{


}

// IMPLEMENT THE INTERRUPT HANDLER
ISR(INT0_vect)
{
   PORTB |= (1<<PB5);

}
ISR(INT1_vect)
{
   PORTB &= (~(1<<PB5));

}
```

So this is the executional interest program in no order, no. So I am building the project. So they believe the sectors will be compiling this done successfully now, connecting what Audrey knows who our what PC, USB port. No, I'm applauding the program to bring about using the icon over here. The program has been successfully uploaded to my order number now, but it is sad to see the output in the hardware that I'm connecting with pertains to digital print to underpin three of my own dinner. And I am going to use the onboard LCD that is present in my order, not foreseeing the output. Now you can see whenever I press the button that is to the development to the on, and maybe in my order, no will be lighted up and let me press the button that is conducted. Three. The onboard LTE will be turned off.

TIMER INTERRUPT MODE FUNCTIONALITY EXPLAINED

In this project, let's pay to understand how the timer works on interrupt or flow more in our microcontrollers. Let's get started. So what does a timer address for a microcontroller that is used for counting them? And some of the basic applications of timers are a great time religion based on my selling frequency of pulses, generating P.W. signals and triggering external devices on peripheral, often microcontrollers. And as I said, time was actually a counter which counts time. There are two methods of counting one this accounting another one is done counting. So accounting is a method of counting from zero to pre-programmed value and doesn't continue as a method of counting from pre-programmed value to zero. And let's understand the working principle of Tamerlan in overflow mode. For that, initially, we will assume the beta value or pre-programmed value to be final and ask when the microcontroller starts, the timer also starts counting from the pre-programmed value at this period. So here we have assembly bills to be filed. So the timer starts counting from five three to six seven eight and it goes on. The maximum value. So this maximum value will be depending on the resolution of the payment, that this may be a payment of 16 bit payment if it's an April payment. The value will be to. It's just nothing but proof of before. And if it gets a 16 bit tamer, the value will be up over 16 with just nothing but six five five three four. So once the timer reaches the maximum value, the timer will roll over from its maximum value to the premium value defined. But it's nothing but fate. So again, once after the fall of payment occurs from the maximum value to the period value. The timer again starts counting from the Peter Valley to its maximum value, and again, the payment falls over. And again, the process continues in time. But this process continues one timer until the timer module stops. So whenever the fall of the time, it occurs from the maximum value to the period value, the payment module will generate an interpreter called timer or flow in which will interpret the processor.

TIMER WORKING PRINCIPLE

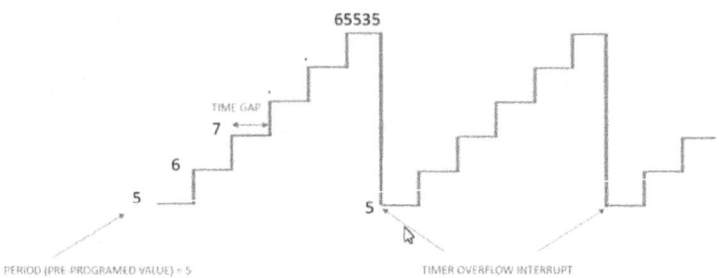

So every time when the timer rollover happens from the maximum value to period value, this will interrupt the processor and we can return a user function for executing a set of lines whenever this roll over of timer happens. So this is how payment works in payment or flow entrapment. So once this even improves the process that we can implement a set of codes written in, say, the saw it off payment workflow vector so that we will see in the programming. But for now, you'll just remember that when our payment rollover happens, the payment will flow in and interrupt the processor. So this interplay will be triggered again and again when the timer rolls over from the maximum value to the period value. So until the cameras stop, this interview will occur again and again when the timer rollover happens. So the timer clock was given by the formula, so some people are basically scaling up. The system clock is nothing but the clock of the microcontroller and is nothing but the number that is used to reduce the frequency of payment. So let's take the minimum value of Priscilla, but this one. So now the timer clock will be equal to this system clock of the microcontroller. Let's say the system clock is 16 megahertz and. Timer Peter was given one by 16 maggots that is equal to sixty two point five nanoseconds. So this is the time, Peter, for one pick of the timer, that is nothing but the. Time up over here. So when the timer clock is equal to 16 megahertz this time gapless sixty two point five nanoseconds. As we calculated here, we will see the configuration port in the next project.

IMPLEMENTING TIMER INTERRUPT PROGRAM IN ARDUINO MICROCONTROLLER

We are just going to see the programming part of implementing timer will flow interest in November ordinal, losing the register level programming. Let's get started. So in the previous project, we just completed our timer, one of our three to eight for generating interest for everyone. Secondly, by lowering the appropriate period value for the timer, as well as setting the predicate out for the timer. And in this project, we are just going to use the onboard LCD of our ordinal board for blinking at a rate of one second, using the timer one or flow into. So I'm just configuring the free Wi-Fi and that is the digital audio output. As we know, when we do spin this country to the onboard enemy of order, no. And inside the ISAF function, I'm just going to write the programming statements that it's used to for toggling this date to be final. So I can write what be. Exalt equal to. One lapse of tough. We are fine. So this line would be all equal to one of a heavy pile if the use of the pot calling the state of the bin whenever this statement is executed, that is initially this low. Executing the statement will make the height that this if initially the business law executing the statement, will make dipping height and independence higher. Initially, this statement will make it law. So likewise, you can use this programming statement for toggling in infants. That's all about the program.

```
// ENABLE THE REQUIRED TIMER INTERRUPT
   TIMSK1 |= (1<<TOIE1);

// SET MODE OF THE TIMER
   TCCR1A &= (~(1<<WGM10)) & (~(1<<WGM11));
   TCCR1B &= (~(1<<WGM12)) & (~(1<<WGM13));

// SET THE PRESCALER FOR THE TIMER
   TCCR1B |= (1<<CS12) | (1<<CS10);
   TCCR1B &= (~(1<<CS11));           //PRESCALAR = 1024

// SET THE PERIOD FOR THE TIMER
   TCNT1 = 49910;   // 1 SECOND
```

```
Invalid library found in C:\Program Files (x86)\Arduino\libraries\Keypad: C:\Program Files (x86)\Arduino\libraries\Keypa
Invalid library found in C:\Program Files (x86)\Arduino\libraries\Keypad: C:\Program Files (x86)\Arduino\libraries\Keypa
No files were added to the sketch.
```

Now you can see whenever the program is starting the process that it will execute all the lines over here, configuring the timer are not going to executing the configuration, but the processor will move to the white look and stay here and probably when the program starts the time of this initiative to forty nine thousand nineteen and the timer is also starting from Fortman thousand p.m. And it will start counting up on when the timer reaches the maximum value of sixty five point three five. The timer rollover happens and the timer will be interrupted by an overflow interrupt and the process will pause all the processes that it was doing here, and it will enter into this sort of function. I didn't say this, I thought it would topple the state of the port and pile on after executing all the lines over here. Processor will be coming back to this wide loop and it will be the same in the process it left here.

Well, the diamond will be also resorted to devalue potatoes and 910, and it will start counting up. Likewise, for every one second. It will be interesting if the processor using overflow interest on this function will be executed, but every one second in the program. So this is called timer interrupt or from metadata, and you can see the onboard L3 present in your order will be blinking at a rate of accurate one second using the timer one or low interrupt. Now I'm building the product using the speaker icon over here. Compilation of success now connects the ordering of the board and then clicks on this icon for uploading the program to what order. Now, the program is fully loaded to the order aboard. No, you need not build any support as we are using only one end that is present in the order. No. And you can see the onboard energy that is present in your order, not just blinking at the top once again using the timer or entered.

TIMER OUTPUT COMPARE MODE FUNCTIONALITY EXPLAINED

let's discuss how a timer works on the output compartment in our area of microcontrollers. Let's get started. So this output compared more of the timer is useful for generating pulses of record frequencies. And let's see how we can generate pulses of required frequency through our output compartment of payments. So let's take the frequency of payment to be 15000 DB hoods, and the time period of the time was given by one by fifteen thousand sixty eight, that is nothing but sixty four microseconds and the time taken for one peak of the timer of sixty four microseconds. And when the timer starts counting from zero, it takes sixty four microseconds for the timer to reach one step. So from zero to one, it takes sixty four microseconds and one to two it takes sixty four microseconds and two to three takes sixty four microseconds. And it goes on. And we are having an output comparison of all microcontrollers. And we will be having another call, the combat register. Which is your sort of father's output compact process, and to this, compared with the stuff, we just want to know that pre-programmed the value. So when the timer starts counting, let's assume the output competition is low. And the timer starts counting from zero when the timer we just don't value to, which is equal to the value that is present in the combat register of the timer. The state of the output competition varies, but initially it was low, so the state of the output competition will become high over here. And this end, an output combat interrupt will interactive process that and using that interest, we will clear the timer count value to zero. So again, no. The timer starts counting from zero. And now you can see we have toggle the state of output competition and now the output competition status height. And the timer counts from zero to one two. And again, when it reaches to. The compromise happens between these two account values and the comparative traveling, so now also the state of the output competition will be toggled, that is. Initially, it was high and now it will become low.

OUTPUT COMPARE

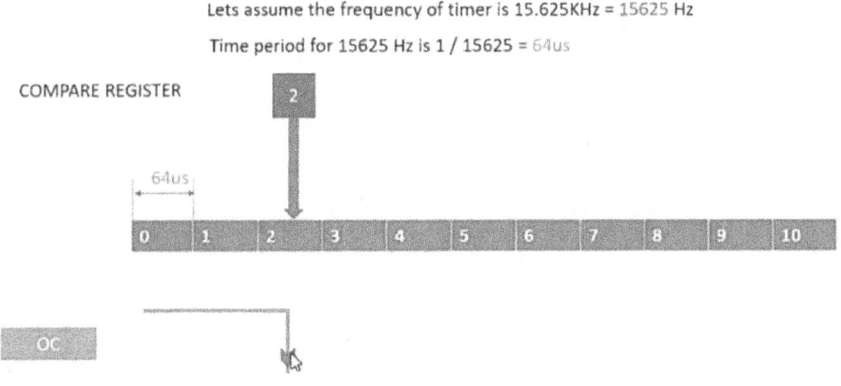

So again, no, the output company model will interrupt the process that I'm using that internally will clear the timer value. Again, no, the timer will start counting from zero and the output compartment will be initially low and it will become high as this process continues. So the on beam of the policies given by 64 microseconds plus 64 plus 64, that is 192 microseconds. And the all famous 192 microseconds in the total time period of the year was given by 192 plus 192. That is 384 microseconds. And thus, by loading the proper appropriate comparator still value we can generate, but it's of required a quiet period of using output, compact enough area microcontroller and thus output compact model of timer in the area of microcontroller is useful for generating pulses of required frequencies.

REGISTER CONFIGURATION FOR TIMER OUTPUT COMPARE MODE IN ARDUINO MICROCONTROLLER

We are just going to configure our time off our adrenal on output compartment using our indestructible programming. Let's get started. So initially, we have three different timers in our audience, about three to eight microcontrollers that are available in our order. No. They are: I'm a zero timer, one timer, too. And let's try to find out what are the output channels available in Nevada at 1.3 to eight. So these are the pinnacle of three to eight. And you can see these are the output compact channels available. We'll see zero and we'll see zero, it'll be on the output compartments for timer zero.

ATMEGA328 - 28 PIN

Arduino function				Arduino function
reset	(PCINT14/RESET) PC6	1 · 28	PC5 (ADC5/SCL/PCINT13)	analog input 5
digital pin 0 (RX)	(PCINT16/RXD) PD0	2 · 27	PC4 (ADC4/SDA/PCINT12)	analog input 4
digital pin 1 (TX)	(PCINT17/TXD) PD1	3 · 26	PC3 (ADC3/PCINT11)	analog input 3
digital pin 2	(PCINT18/INT0) PD2	4 · 25	PC2 (ADC2/PCINT10)	analog input 2
digital pin 3 (PWM)	(PCINT19/OC2B/INT1) PD3	5 · 24	PC1 (ADC1/PCINT9)	analog input 1
digital pin 4	(PCINT20/XCK/T0) PD4	6 · 23	PC0 (ADC0/PCINT8)	analog input 0
VCC	VCC	7 · 22	GND	GND
GND	GND	8 · 21	AREF	analog reference
crystal	(PCINT6/XTAL1/TOSC1) PB6	9 · 20	AVCC	VCC
crystal	(PCINT7/XTAL2/TOSC2) PB7	10 · 19	PB5 (SCK/PCINT5)	digital pin 13
digital pin 5 (PWM)	(PCINT21/OC0B/T1) PD5	11 · 18	PB4 (MISO/PCINT4)	digital pin 12
digital pin 6 (PWM)	(PCINT22/OC0A/AIN0) PD6	12 · 17	PB3 (MOSI/OC2A/PCINT3)	digital pin 11 (PWM)
digital pin 7	(PCINT23/AIN1) PD7	13 · 16	PB2 (SS/OC1B/PCINT2)	digital pin 10 (PWM)
digital pin 8	(PCINT0/CLKO/ICP1) PB0	14 · 15	PB1 (OC1A/PCINT1)	digital pin 9 (PWM)

And we'll see one neat and we'll see one be on the output compartments for timer one. And we'll see output compression and what they might do. And we are just going to configure the output channel of timer one for this purpose, so you can see these are the steps that need to be implemented for configuring the timer on one of our microcontrollers in the output compartment. So I'm copying all these steps I've been pasting in the other. Let's implement these steps one by one, and initially you can see the first two steps. We just want to enable the global internet. But. As I said in the previous projects, this must be enabled by using any inputs in your microcontroller military to it. So this can be done by calling the fountain. Yes, right. So calling this function will enable the IG Nobel but as mentioned in the previous projects. And the next step was we just want to enable that one time and. So going to our dataset. Under this timer, one, go to the register, this person. You can see. We'll see one meet that is available to be a mosquito start. This bill does nothing but this time counter one output company met in any bill, so for enabling the interview for John and of timer one, you just want to enable this. But if you are using Channel B, you just want to enable this bit. So I'm enabling this, but the union must give one or equal to one, and so we'll see i.e. one eight. On the next steps, we just want to see more of the timer. So here also, I just want bitumen one to be running in normal mode, so that can be said by using the table over here as we did in the last unforgiveness mixture. We are just going to clear all this for which wd am pinto wd 13 bits. So these two bits and then 11 are available in the PCC. Aveni under column 13 are available in the PCC, R1 B Register. So I'm going to the PCC Aveni. I will clear it.

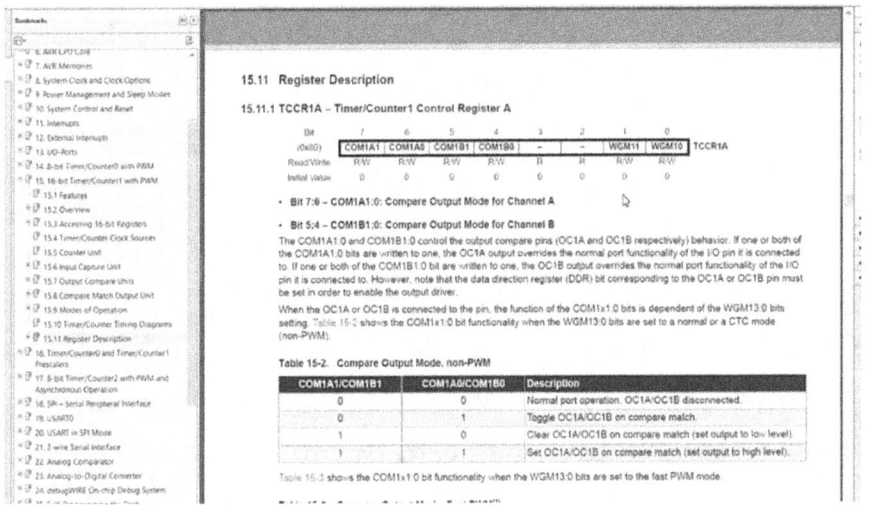

W0 been. And. WD am 11. And going to the beach is the odd one, I will clear all the pain. So this will set the time, a lot of money and more. On the mix, just a plus, we just want to compare output more so this can be settled, you're the bits. Common is it uncommon, even off base the Aveni? So if you are using B, you must contract these two topics since I'm using John and I'm configuring these two bits. So you may give a value of zero zero. The output combat channel will be disabled if I give a value of zero one to these two bits of down and you will be anchored in the compartment. And if you're the value of one zero, it will clear B or C one NI on the compartment. And if I give you the value of one one, this one is set to B or C one NI on the compartment. So I just want this to be happening in or see one. So I'm setting the second one to zero and I'm creating Nic on one given. So going to the PGC when?

I'm sitting there. One is Edo. And I'M on one. One. So this will all be we'll see one near ultracompact channel on kompromat on next thing that we just want to set the free scale up for tomorrow. So here also, I just want the prince to be one zero to four as we configured in the timer ledger. So for that, we will be using these three system levels and tools. So I just want to say Celestial Unci has been clearing this year's 11 for the country, getting the pre-schooler to be one zero two four. So going to the odd one, we. I will be sitting. See you all. See, often. Creating the. See, it's 11. So this will configure the police killer to be one zero two four.

```
// SET THE COMPARE OUTPUT MODE
TCCR1A |= (1<<COM1A0);
TCCR1A &= (~(1<<COM1A1);   // TOGGLE

// SET THE PRESCALER FOR THE TIMER
TCCR1B |= (1<<CS12) | (1<<CS10);
TCCR1B &= (~(1<<CS11));    // PRE = 1024

// START THE TIMER WITH INITIAL VALUE


// LOAD THE PERIOD FOR THE TIMER

// CONFIGURE THE OUTPUT COMPARE PIN AS O/P

// IMPLEMENT THE ISR FUCNTION
```

Next, we just want to start the timer with the initial value, so we know the timer count registers nothing but B, C and

B one. So I'm providing the initial value. Zero, two, B, C and D one. And the next step is we just want to find the appropriate immediate value for the output company registered so that the compromise happens for every second in no time at all for the microcontroller. That is, we just want to calculate the bit of value in such a way that for every second in our microcontroller, the compromise happens between the time value and the output components to value. So our system, Glaucus, is keeping my guards and the timer clock was given by 16 maggots, one zero two four, that is to please Kayla. So the timer clock will be fifteen thousand six twenty four years and the time for one pick of the time minutes given by impulse of fifteen thousand six hundred sixty four microseconds. So the sixty four microseconds is nothing but the time taken for one peak of the timer or the time taken for the timer. 41 count. So the time gap, it's not sixty four microseconds. So we just want to find the appropriate period value for which the payment takes exactly one second counting up to that median value. So that can be done by dividing a thousand milliseconds by one peak of the timer. This thousand millisecond is nothing but the one second under sixty four microseconds is nothing but the one taking off the timer. So dividing these two will give the results of ten thousand six twenty five. So this is the count value for the timer for exactly one second bullet, so we can directly load this value to the output compared with the stuff we know the output number registered for channel in our timer. We'll see Aveni and for Channel B zero distress or C or wouldn't be. So I'm lowering the value to the or Aveni to be 15000 625. And next, two things we just want to configure the output competitiveness output. We know that we are just going to use this nasty output competition.

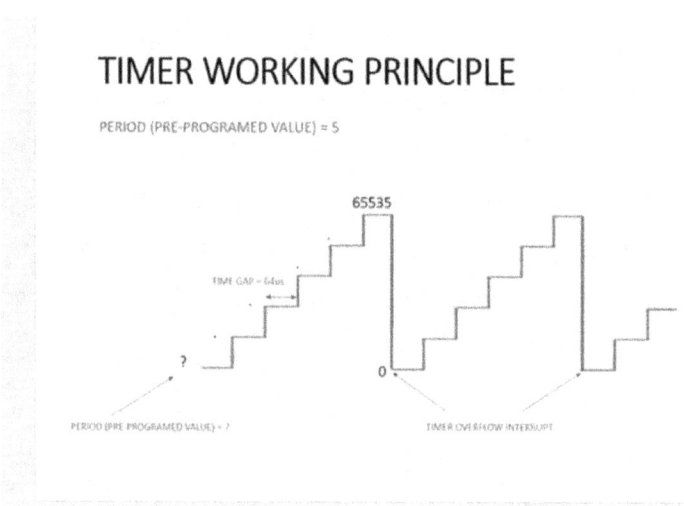

So I just want to configure the B-1s output. That can be done by setting the. Be one big tough B B R religion, this will configure D output, compact business output. And the next thing that we want to do is we just want to implement the HSR function. So the answer for dimer one output commodities, motorists, I have sort of. Remember one? Compare. But so this is the ISI function for payment, one in the output compartment and inside this ISI. I just want to do two things. That is one I will clear the timer count value to be zero on next. I will reload the output compared to just the initial value. That is nothing, but I will load the Brooklyn Dodgers 623 as the value put on the combat register. But we did initially. So that is all about the conflict isn't part of our combat in our time on one. Let's implement the programming part in the next project.

GENERATING PULSES USING TIMER OUTPUT COMPARE MODE IN ARDUINO MICROCONTROLLER

We're just going to implement the program of output combat in no order, not using our register level programming. So in the previous project, we just configured the timer, one of our microcontrollers, at three to eight in the output compartment. Let's try to understand this programming logic, and we will implement this program in hardback. When the program starts, the processor executes all the lines over here, and it will enter into this loop. And it will stay here, since this is an infinite loop on pardon me, when the program starts, the payment also starts from zero when this line is executed. So the timer will be counting up enough that exactly one second, the timer will be to the count value of Pinto, some 625, as we calculated in the previous project. And when it reaches four thousand six twenty five at that moment, this timer count value will be equal to the output compared with the value. So whenever this compromise happens between output combat register and timer count value, this based on the output compartment that is the data we be one that this we'll see.

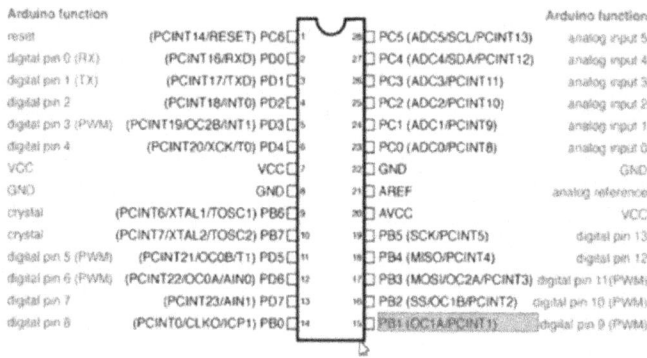

What happens will be toggled as we configured in the last project. So we just configured these two bits for toggling in the last project. So the state of the P.B. one will toggle that is, initially, if it was low, it will become high input to us, i.e. it will become low. So the state of the pin will be toggled after that timer. One model of a one microcontroller will be interpreting the processor using the output compact interface. So the process of process, all the process that it was doing here and it will come to this iron start function coming to this, I thought function. The process will be executing all the lines over here. That way, it will clear the timer count value to zero. And it will reload the output. Compare this value to the initial value 15 percent to certify that we have already loaded here. So after executing all the lines over here, the processor comes back to this wide loop and it will resume the process. It will appear. So now again, as we have reloaded this value to be zero, the timer will be counting up from zero and after one second, it will again reach this fifteen thousand six hundred five. And this process continues in the timer and then the output compartment. So this is the routine of the timer output combat program and for every one second, the state of the output compartment will be toggled. So we will be connecting a little to the pre one bin of the three to eight. That is the digital opinion of Audrey. No. And you can see for every one second, the lady will be toggling it fake. Ripest, the lady will be blinking at a rate of one second, using this time on one output company model. So that's all about the program. I hope now we are clear with the programming logic. Now I'm building the program using the equation over here.

Sorry, I just left one bracket here. Now I'm building again. Now, connect your adrenal bowl to your USB port of the PC. Once you have connected the order, no. Click on this item icon to upload the program to you. What are they? And the program has been successfully uploaded to you, what order number? No, Bill, this sergeant, to see the output in the hardware. That is, you just want to connect the panel of a lady to the digital print to order north through open to register on Ellie, you just want to connect it to ground of order. Not. And you can see the lady will be blinking at a rate of one second using the timer.

TIMER INPUT CAPTURE MODE FUNCTIONALITY EXPLAINED

let's try to understand the timer input capstone module of every other microcontroller. Let's get started. So most often this input captain module is useful for finding the frequency of signals produced to the input captured. So let's take this example, an application for understanding the working principle of this input captain module. So the frequency is measured by counting the number of clock pulses appearing. So let's see how we can find this frequency. I assume that the system clock of 16 megahertz and the preschoolers, those on 24 and the timer clock is given by 16 maggots developed by one zero two four, that's 15000 625 hertz. And when the timer starts, the timer starts counting from zero and it will start counting up and the time period of the timer given by inverse of the fourteen thousand six hundred sixty four microseconds. So this time, Peter, that's nothing but the time taken for one pick of the day . For each count of the timer, the timer picks 64 microseconds, not just for counting from zero to one. It takes sixty four microseconds. And in a similar way, for each count, the timer takes sixty four microseconds. And we will be having an input to bring in our microcontroller. And we will be having a captain register. For storing values in our microcontroller. So let's see how this input gadget is employed in finding the frequency of. So whenever rising, think pulses given to the input capture to be microcontroller, the corresponding timer count value at that moment that is in this moment, you can see the timer count values to. So the corresponding timer count value at that moment will be stored in the capture register. So in the similar way, the pulse goes on, and when the next two, it occurs in the input Carter pin. Because funding on the value of the payment will be noted in the capital register.

INPUT CAPTURE

System clock 16MHz & prescaler 1024 so timer clock = 16MHz / 1024 = 15625 Hz
Lets assume the frequency of timer is 15.625KHz = 15625 Hz
Time period for 15625 Hz is 1 / 15625 = 64us

He had a six, so they value six loaders to the captain register, so you can see this is a complete pulse. This is the one time under 60 of Ping. So you can see this is the start of this pulse and this one is the start of the next pulse. So we got the corresponding countervailing form one complete pulse. So when it's a break, these two values. I'm getting four counts. Six minus two this fall. So we know for each count the time it takes sixty four microseconds and for four counts, the time period is sixty four microseconds into four. That is six microseconds. So this 256 microsecond is nothing but the time period of this complete wave, right? So from this?In this one, the time, Peter, this 256 microsecond. So we got this time period of the review and for finding the frequency we can invert this 256 microsecond. So one by 256 microseconds, three thousand nine or six point two hearts. So this is the frequency of pulse given to the input. So does the frequency of pulses do using the input captain or timer in any of your microcontrollers? And also, whenever this right thing, it balances given to the input counterspin input cattle interest will deposit that this can be further and for many applications in the work program. So I hope now you understood the working principle of input captured using an example of my sitting frequency of pulses.

MEASURING TIME DURATION OF PULSE USING TIMER INPUT CAPTURE MODE IN ARDUINO

We just configured the input caps mode of timer one in our ordinal. Now in this project next I will implement the program in our hardware. So in our order, we have a serial monitor. This order, no I.D. It has a serial monitor for opening it. Click on this set take on. You can see this is the seating monitor. You will receive the Citadel monitor only when you can if you're ordering a board, who knew what it was before, you can see I have collected my order number for the country of my USB port, so it is highlighting the company. So we are just going to utilize this serial monitor for printing the data that we receive from the input, and get it registered over time instead of using an LCD. I'm going to use this serial monitor. I'm closing this. We can initiate this serial monitor by giving it a pen board rate for the city and monitor that can be done by writing Serial Dot Begin. And in the process, you just want to go. Anybody? I'm giving 9600. So now using this line, I'm just initiating the Syrian monitor 9600 more. You can see these are the varieties of warheads you can give anybody, depending on what it's. And after that, inside the HSR function, I'm just going to print the value of the variable captured to the scene and monitor for that. I can carry a lot. Friend. Captured. After that, I'm just going to. But in. Max Larson. This is nothing but internal. So after printing the value of captured data, this line will bring the country to the next line for printing mid-next data. So that is why I'm giving this. So that is all about the program. Now you can see when the program starts.

```
unsigned int captured = 0;
void setup()
{
    // ENABLE THE GLOBAL INTERRUPT ENABLE BIT
    sei();

    // ENABLE THE REQUIRED TIMER INTERRUPT
    TIMSK1 |= (1<<ICIE1);

    // SET MODE OF THE TIMER
    TCCR1A &= (~(1<<WGM10)) & (~(1<<WGM11));
    TCCR1B &= (~(1<<WGM12)) & (~(1<<WGM13));   // NORMAL

    // SET THE PRESCALER FOR THE TIMER
    TCCR1B |= (1<<CS10) | (1<<CS12);
    TCCR1B &= (~(1<<CS11));      // PRE = 1024

    // START THE TIMER WITH INITIAL VALUE
    TCNT1 = 0;
```

Global variables use 9 bytes (0%) of dynamic memory, leaving 2039 bytes for local variables. Maximum is 2048 bytes.
Invalid library found in C:\Program Files (x86)\Arduino\libraries\Keypad: C:\Program Files (x86)\Arduino\libraries
Invalid library found in C:\Program Files (x86)\Arduino\libraries\Keypad: C:\Program Files (x86)\Arduino\libraries

The processor will execute all the lines over here on one set to execute this line. The timer will start counting from zero and it will start counting up. And after doing all the lines, the process will be. Held in this wide loop with dissent in place, look. And this time I will be counting up and it will be reaching 6.3 feet, its maximum value after reaching the maximum value. The timer will roll over to zero. And after that, it will start counting from zero. So this process continues in timer and it will do this process again and again until the timer at stop. And regarding the programming logic we have configured to be input kept captive in racing and captain mode, and we are connecting a pause button to the input captain BP zero. That is the digital pin eight of ordinal. So whenever I press this button, I think it's pulse will be given to the input of the pin.

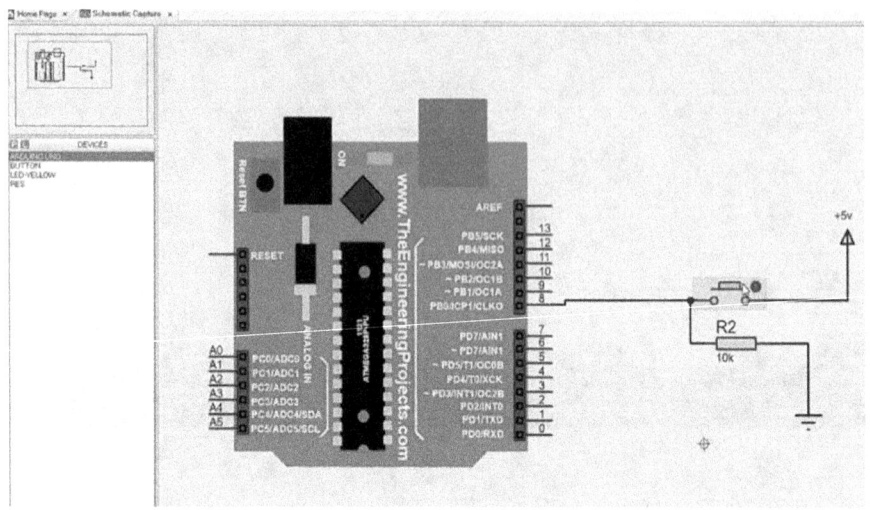

And whenever I release this button following its pulse will be given to the input captain that is digital tape. And whenever I give it, I think it's pulse to the input, capturing a pin by pressing this button. This time on, one will be interesting, the professor using the input captured in prayer and the process that passes all the process that it was doing here, and it will come to this by itself. So it will be excluding all the links that are available here. That is, it will store the input cap, the register value where a variable is called capture, and after that it will be printing the variable captor to the serial monitor. And then it will be going to the next claiming the serial number and not executing all the three names. It will be coming back to this wide loop and it will be resuming the process. It reappears. So this is the routine of the input capture program, and whenever we press this button with this contact will be an input capture pin. Raising its pulse will be given to the input capture channel of time on one and the corresponding input capture register value will be stored in the capture register and the capture registered value will be printed to the serial monitor. And after that, enter will be given to the serial monitor Annapolis reporting all the lines over here. The control will be coming to this wide loop. So this is the return of the input capture program. So in a similar way, you can use some mathematical and logical calculations for capturing simultaneously two values, but finding the frequency of pulses using those input capture modules. As we learned in the Input Capital Working Project, we can find the frequency of pulses using this input capture. So I'm building this project, you're saying the big one over here. Sorry, I left one correct. Sorry, I left one bracket here. Now I'm building the project again. Now, the compilation is successful. I have already corrected my order number to my USB port, so I'm uploading the program to my order now using the icon over here. And the program has been successfully uploaded to my order, no. No, but it is scheduled. And after building the schedule correctly, our Yunel to the USB port of your PC through a USB cable. And using this icon on the top right corner of the window, you can open this little monitor of no I.D.. So this is the Syrian trough or. And you can see whenever I pressed the button that is guaranteed to be zero of three to eight, the timer value at that moment will be stored to the variable called captured and then the capture variable value will be printed to the serial monitor with the enter at the end. And now I'm pressing the button that is counter to digital print to order. No, and now you can see the timer count value that is available in the captured variable is printed to the serial monitor. And as the program starts, you can see the timer count value starts from zero and it reaches the maximum value six five eight three five. And this is the purpose of the timer. It will start from zero and it will reach the maximum value. And again, it will come back to the floor and it will count up.

PWM (PULSE WIDTH MODULATION) FUNCTIONALITY EXPLAINED

We're just going to see our P.W. on books in any microcontroller. Peatlands are nothing but piles of moralism, as the name says. We are just going to bury the bulk with but controlling the power delivery to any circuit. So some of the applications of petroleum are workplace regulation, and there's some obvious brightness adjustment in Liddy's speed control of the motor. So most probably these VW signals are given to the gift of the MOSFET for controlling the power to the circuit. So these BW waves are generated in a particular frequency. Let's stick or assume the frequency to be one Hertz if the frequency is one Hertz, the time period is given one by one by frequency. So the time period is one second. So if you are telling the time period, time period means.

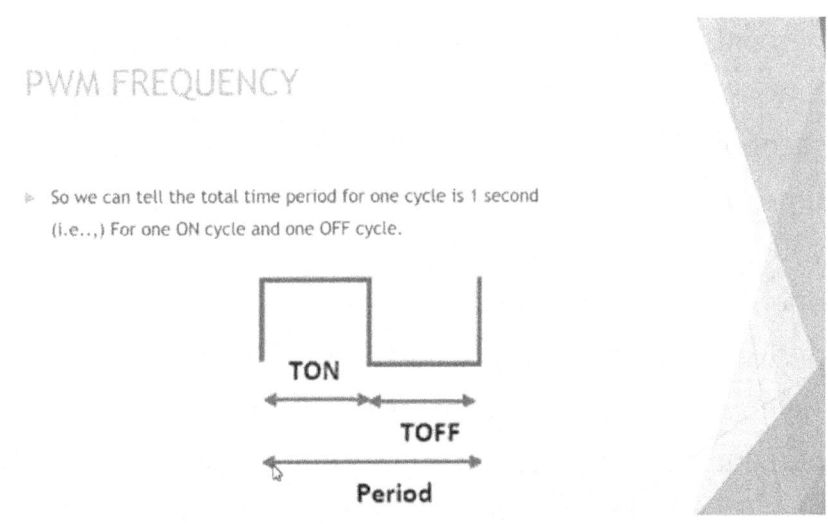

One cycle of DPW will be this, including the B on one B of ATV, so this PDA is named this time period. So this beta once again for one hertz. And this be on is the. On beam of the beam on this beat of a sea of beam of David. Let's see our microcontrollers operating in a fable. Then this beyond is the firewall signal, and the 50 zero will signal if your motor control is operating in 3.3 world, then to be honest, 3.3 and the office zero world. So what defines this beyond time? This one is defined by it, don't call it a cycle. So what did you say? Let's take beyond fitted as defined by a term. So if I give up the duty cycle of 50 percent, it means one puts frequency. We know this time period is. One second. So 50 percent off one second will be beyond pain. 50 percent off once again, this one, five seconds. So one in five seconds on bang and pointless seconds of fame will be delivered, so you forgive the ridiculous 10 percent it then for one hertz frequency. We know the time, Peter just one second. So in percentage of one second, this point one second, so point one second on time on point nine second of payments delivered. And if you give the due to cyclase 30 percent, it's 30 percent off one second. Its derivatives are on and 70 percent is derivatives. Still, that is point three seconds on, one point seven seconds off. If you are 70 percent secular, then 70 percent is off one second. At this point, seven seconds on and 30 percent it's remaining this off. No, we just got to know the duty cycle before and beyond and beyond the period of the AWB. So no, we will just paper call the power delivery. So let's assume the microcontroller is delivering the petroleum and firewall signal. So if I give people a solid duty cycle, then the voltage at the pin will be because people's fuel needs are 2.8 world.

T_{on} & T_{off}

- T_{on} period time is defined by the term Duty Cycle.
- If I give Duty cycle as 50%, It means for 1Hz frequency, 0.5s On & 0.5s Off
- If I give Duty cycle as 10%, It means for 1Hz frequency, 0.1s On & 0.9s Off
- If I give Duty cycle as 30%, It means for 1Hz frequency, 0.3s On & 0.7s Off
- If I give Duty cycle as 70%, It means for 1Hz frequency, 0.7s On & 0.3s Off

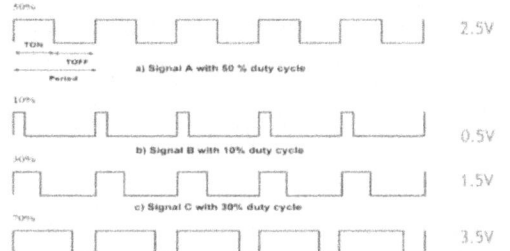
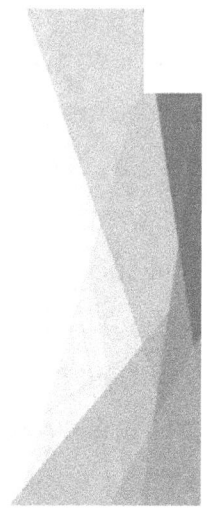

And if they do, the cycle is 10 percent it, then the beyond famous 10 percent is so the percentage of fuel that is 0.5 work will be the output of the BW will. So if they do disclose 30 percent of it, then the beyond pain will be 30 percent. So the output will be 30 percent of fivefold that this 1.5 world and if they do basically 70 percent it, then the output will be 70 percent of fuel. That is 3.5. What if we are using a 3.3 watt microcontroller? Then this power will be also very. So let's take another example. Let's assume, no, we are generating a political wave of thousands the time, but it is given by one thousand that this one millisecond. So the period now was one millisecond. And we will try to assume that it is cycles and the power to revert to the circular. So beyond that, as defined by the to cycle. If people are sending the signal, then for that frequency 4.9 millisecond on and one five millisecond of its delivery. So the power to revert to the sacredness of people's needs of firewood that is 2.4, you would if you had to do the cycle has been percent it. It means four thousand hertz frequency. One one millisecond is 1.9 milliseconds off. If you do two cycles, 30 percent, 30 percent of one millisecond is on time. That is 0.3 milliseconds on time and 0.7 milliseconds often. And if fact it is circular, 70 percent it means four thousand hertz. Some people snapped off one millisecond on that point, some milliseconds on and point three milliseconds off. So for 10 percent, is the poverty level, this 10 percent is the end of the world, but this point for the world and 30 percent, it's about 30 percent of the world. That is 1.4 you work and for 70 percent, it is on people's minds of 3.5. All this the poverty level. So now I hope you got an idea about P.W. and some of the basic parameters of BWL, such as duty cycle frequency, time period beyond beef. So we will see in the next project.

REGISTER CONFIGURATION FOR PWM SIGNAL GENERATION IN ARDUINO MICROCONTROLLER

We are just going to configure our output computer module of timer one in our ordinal for generating VW lists using the registered level programming. Let's get started. So we know that in timer one, not over Adriano, we have two different output compartments. As I said before, these output compartments can be useful for generating BW movies. So we are just going to use this channel real time on one that outputs a compact channel of timer one for generating BW waves of 250 kilowatts. Initially, there are seven steps for. Generating BW Signal, you'll think of a timer, one model of over 16 microcontrollers. So for us to step, we just want to set the mode of the payment. As we know, that can be settled using these for, but that this WD 32 W3m 10 bits. So you can see in the stable if these four bits are having the value. Five, six, seven, 14 or 15, this timer is centered in Boston P.W. model that this if I'm providing a value of zero one zero one to these four bits that will set the detainment of two P.W. a bit.

FROM THE DATASHEET - TCCR1A & B REGISTER

Table 47. Waveform Generation Mode Bit Description[1]

Mode	WGM13	WGM12 (CTC1)	WGM11 (PWM11)	WGM10 (PWM10)	Timer/Counter Mode of Operation	TOP	Update of OCR1X	TOV1 Flag Set on
0	0	0	0	0	Normal	0xFFFF	Immediate	MAX
1	0	0	0	1	PWM, Phase Correct, 8-bit	0x00FF	TOP	BOTTOM
2	0	0	1	0	PWM, Phase Correct, 9-bit	0x01FF	TOP	BOTTOM
3	0	0	1	1	PWM, Phase Correct, 10-bit	0x03FF	TOP	BOTTOM
4	0	1	0	0	CTC	OCR1A	Immediate	MAX
5	0	1	0	1	Fast PWM, 8-bit	0x00FF	BOTTOM	TOP
6	0	1	1	0	Fast PWM, 9-bit	0x01FF	BOTTOM	TOP
7	0	1	1	1	Fast PWM, 10-bit	0x03FF	BOTTOM	TOP
8	1	0	0	0	PWM, Phase and Frequency Correct	ICR1	BOTTOM	BOTTOM
9	1	0	0	1	PWM, Phase and Frequency Correct	OCR1A	BOTTOM	BOTTOM
10	1	0	1	0	PWM, Phase Correct	ICR1	TOP	BOTTOM
11	1	0	1	1	PWM, Phase Correct	OCR1A	TOP	BOTTOM
12	1	1	0	0	CTC	ICR1	Immediate	MAX
13	1	1	0	1	Reserved	-	-	-
14	1	1	1	0	Fast PWM	ICR1	BOTTOM	TOP
15	1	1	1	1	Fast PWM	OCR1A	BOTTOM	TOP

And if it is having a value of six, that is zero one one zero. Boston of them nine. But the selected and and it is having a value of zero one one one. Boston P.W. a member is selected for this, having a value of triple one zero loss to the selected, and if it is having a value of double one, double one again ought to be the private sector. So what we will do is I'm just going to set these four books in Boston, P.W. 10 bit. So I just want to say to them. WD 11 and 10. And they want to clear the WD 30. That is I'm just going to give a value of seven to these four, but. We know that from the dataset, this WD 10 and 11 is available in the basic Aveni Register and Column 13 is available in the PCC and wouldn't be registered. So I am. Searching for Lebanon bin and then clearing the debris, Jim, 30. So this line will clear the WD 30. And this line will be WD and between pieces, the odd Ottoman be registered. And this line will sell to the WD young bin and 11 percent Armani registered. So we have it configured. The timer won an Oscar p.w and bit more.

```
Debug  [*] Untitled3  TIMER_PWM.c
   1        // SET MODE OF THE TIMER
   2        TCCR1B &= ~(1<<WGM13);
   3        TCCR1B |= (1<<WGM12);
   4        TCCR1A |= (1<<WGM10) | (1<<WGM11);    // FAST PWM 10 BIT
   5
   6        // SET PWM MODE
   7
   8
   9
  10        // SET THE PRESCALER FOR THE TIMER FOR SETTING PWM FREQUENCY
  11
  12
  13        // CONFIGURE THE OUTPUT COMPARE PIN AS O/P
  14
  15
  16        //SET THE DUTY CYCLE
```

And the next step was we just want to say to the BW mode. So in no time, we have two different BW modes. They are. Inverting BW, more inverting BW model that can be subtle, using the comb one even and comb one is little bits of PCC Albany Register can see. These two are the. But. That is useful for setting DPW more.

FROM THE DATASHEET - TCCR1A REGISTER

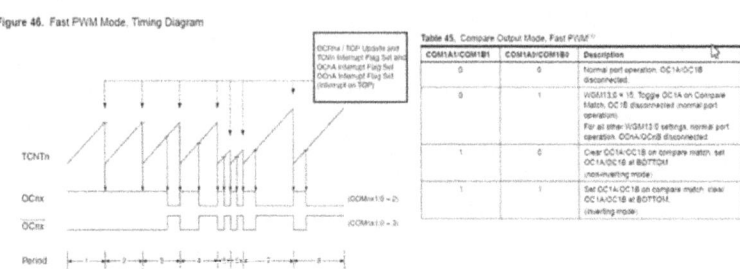

You must know that the output compare pin of the timer one is only generating the BWB, so we will use only the channels of the output compartment for generating P.W. So if you are using this channel ye of time on one, you can use these two bits that is column one year one and column one is equal for completing the complete output more. And if you are using this Channel B, then you just want to use this one with zero on one B one for configuring the combat output model that is for possible problem. That is why we are using these two, but that the second one even uncommon is it. So there are two modes of problem in over time. Our one model one is non-voting mode. Another one is inverting mode, so you face a value of one zero. So this common event is uncommon is that one is said to be pre deployment, non inverting mode. And if they set the value to one one, this will set the problem in inverting mode. So let's understand these two modes one by one. So initially, when the timer starts, as we sat past problems and 10 bit more, the timer will count from zero and it will reach maximum value to power and that this one zero two three once it reaches one zero two three. It will fall down to zero, and again it will contain one to three. And this process continues in time. And as we know, the output company model is useful for generating the problem in over time on one. We will be loading our pre-programmed value or the output combat register that this will see Aveni register. So let's understand the inverting mode of problem generation. So as I said, let's assume the output company register is having a value of five to one month as the timer starts from zero DPW pin. That is, the output compartment will become high at that moment and when the timer starts counting up and when it reaches deep value five one. At that moment, the timer count value is now equal to the output company registered value. So at this moment, the output of the BW pin will become low. The timer counts up, and when it reaches one zero two three, the timer will fall to zero. At this moment, the Freedom Olympian will again become hype and this process continues and the events will be generated as part of this vital value for our lives and the output compelled to do so in non inverting mode. The duty cycle of the P.W. Male is defined by the value program in the Ultimate Combat Register, so this value that is given in the output combat register must be between zero to one zero two three. That is from zero percentage to underrepresented. And let's come to the second mode, which is the inverse of not inverting murderous inverting mode in this mode. All the same, except that once when the timer starts counting from zero, the P.W. spin will become low. And when a compromise happens between the timer value and the competitors' value, the petroleum bin will become high and it will remain high till the timer reaches value. One zero two three Once it reaches one zero two three, DPW will become law and this process continues. And the problem will be generated in this method and we will be using only the non inverting mode. So I'm just going to say common even, and I will clear the common, is it all so I have said today not involving more than P.W. Next, please, we just want to set the price killer for the. Played out on frequency, so I have decided to generate BW waves of proof of petulance. So my. System clock frequency is 16 maggots. But achieving. 250 kilohertz. I just want to set please kill it off. Sixty four. As we know. 16 megahertz. There will be 64. Will give me 250 kilohertz. So for setting that, we just want to go to the. PCC Irwin, DE-register. We're going to see these three will certainly please the killer for our timer so far, certainly for his killer of 64. I just want to say. So, yes, 11 and 16 bit. And I just want to clear this as well, but I just want to provide a value of zero one one to these three, but so I am doing that. I have

Satyadeep, please scale out file 64. That is, we are generating alarm signals of frequency to have big loads. So the next step was we just want to configure the output in this output that does nothing but. This baby one must be configured as output for generating DPW, so that can be done by inserting the baby one bit of baby arbiter. So this will configure the output combat on an ill timer one as output. And the next step was we just want to set the nuclear cycle for the BWB, as it said. We are just going to use be known inwardly. Being more of 3W and in would be more whatever value that we are going to give to the output compared register will be the on team of the BW distributors. So if they give the value of FY12 to the Orsi, outwardly, that is the output compared with the star of Primer one, then 50 percent below the cycle is achieved. And if they do, the value of one zero to three hundred percent duty cycle institute. So you can do any values between zero to one zero two three four achieving would be cyclo zero percent. It's still under personnage. So we will try to program our audience for them, but I think BW means 250 kilowatts in the upcoming project.

GENERATING PULSES OF REQUIRED FREQUENCY AND DUTY CYCLE USING PWM IN ARDUINO

let's take the program over Arduino for generating beats in waves of big loads. Let's get started. So in the previous project, we just wanted our output computer model of timer one for generating redoubling waves up over big loads. I'm copying all this code. And I think it ought to be set up. Actually, what we are going to do is we are just going to connect that reality to the baby, one that is the output compact channel of the timer one. And we are just going to vary its brightness from the minimum to maximum and then from maximum to minimum. And we are just going to continue this process in a routine manner. So for hearing the brightness of LCD, we are just going to use the beauty of VW. As I mentioned in the previous project, the value given to the OCR when comparing the star will be fine. The beauty cycle of DPW. It can be from zero to one zero two three. Wearing it, you can take it from zero plus to another person. So what I will do is inside the wide loop. I will write. Toulouse. One look will be running from zero to. One zero, two three.

```
// SET THE PRESCALER FOR THE TIMER FOR SETTING PWM FREQUENCY
// FREQ OF PWM = 16MHz / 64 = 250KHz
  TCCR1B |= (1<<CS10) | (1<<CS11);
  TCCR1B &= ~(1<<CS12);              // PRESCALER = 64

// CONFIGURE THE OUTPUT COMPARE PIN AS O/P
  DDRB |= (1<<DDB1);


}

void loop()
{
  for(i=0;i<1024
    // SET THE DUTY CYCLE
    OCR1A = 0-1023;   //100%

}
```

```
Global variables use 184 bytes (8%) of dynamic memory, leaving 1864 by
Invalid library found in C:\Program Files (x86)\Arduino\libraries\Keyp
Invalid library found in C:\Program Files (x86)\Arduino\libraries\Keyp
```

But one zero two three. He said that clue. I will be providing the value of B or C ordering me to be I. And for each value. I'm giving you no millisecond delay. And after the look I'm giving. It also can. And after this, Billy. I'm just going to write another loop. Wits will be running from one zero two three to. Zero. In descending order. So now you can see this first look will be running from zero to one zero two three. And it will be giving the values from zero to one zero two three to the old or one register with two millisecond delay for each one. So the duty cycle of the BWB will be increasing from zero percentage to understand it, with two millisecond delay for each value. Once they do this, they could be just in maximum value one day or two three hours. Once the duty cycle is hundred percent it, it will stay at 100 percent each for two seconds. And after this two second delay, this loop will be running on. This loop will reduce this cycle from under postnatal zero percent. But that is, it will be running from one zero two three two zero in descending order. This will also give the value to the we'll see our evidence started with that time interval of two milliseconds for each value and once it reaches the minimum value zero, but some date or the minimum value of zero, it will stay in zero for two seconds. That is, the duty cycle will be paying and zero for two seconds. And after two seconds, this loop will be landing as these two loops are given in, say, the infinite loop. So initially, the lady will be turned off on this look, will be wearing its brightness from minimum to maximum, and it will be staying in maximum for two seconds and after two seconds, this look will be running on. This look will be varying its brightness from maximum to minimum enough that it reaches the minimum value or after it is postponed, or it will stay in office for two seconds. And after that, it will be varying from minimum to maximum. And this Robin continues. So that is all about the programming logic. No, you just want to be Gladys. I am a variable. So I am declaring that.

```
sketch_apr24a §

}

void loop()
{
   for(i=0;i<1024;i++)
      {
         OCR1A = i;   //100%
         delay(2);
      }
      delay(2000);

   for(i=1023;i<0;i--)
      {
         OCR1A = i;   //100%
         delay(2);
      }
      delay(2000);
```

```
Done uploading
Global variables use 184 bytes (8%) of dynamic
Invalid library found in C:\Program Files (x86)
Invalid library found in C:\Program Files (x86)
```

Now the programming is complete now, click on this icon for compiling this sketch. Now, the compilation is successful. No character ordering a boat to you, whether you will be a port of the PC through a USB cable, once connected, click on the arrow icon for uploading the program to your adrenal. Now the program is successfully uploaded to her adrenal. No, build the good to see the output in the harbor. That is correct. And they need to be free. We want that timer one output compartment, which is nothing but the digital pin nine ordinal. So we are using a 221B register for connecting and all of the energy to digital, benign or not, unlike a lot of entities, can't get to the ground of ordinal. Once the statue was built, power up your order, no using a power adapter, audio thing, you must be a port of the PC. Now you can see the LCD that is granted digital benign order. No, this rating is based on the duty cycle of the DPW mills generator.

ANALOG TO DIGITAL CONVERTOR WORKING EXPLAINED

We are just going to see our in model looks into the microcontroller and what instrument that is using by converting analog signal to digital signals. Let's get started. So what does the sensor? Sensors are tiny components that is useful for converting any physical parameters into electric signals. So the different types of sensors at. Temperature, humidity, oppressive smoke, gas, proximity, air, that's green and MetallDoctor. So the parameters may vary, but the main purpose of sensor is to say, let's take the example of temperature. The temperature signal that is available in the environment is converted to equal electric signals. Your guess of humanity The Moisture content available in the air is converted to equal electric signals that can be sensed using any microcontroller. And depending on the. Type of output that it is giving defense outside, consecrated to two types, one analog sends up another one this beautiful sensor. So let's understand what are these two? First one is Bechdel's and set a very good example of a digital sensors, a proximity sensor, so we will be having three points by world drone and output and we must it if I will come down here and it will probably output through the spin. And when they place any object in this sensing region of the sensor. This output bin will become high that it will provide a final signal, this output bin and when they remove that object, this will give a zero world signal in this bill.

Digital Sensor

So this is working off the digital sense that when this insight is sensed, it will give a high signal or low signal depending on the sensor we are using. And when the object is removed, it will give a low signal. In the output bin, it has only two values of output on a site. Another one is low. The second papers and a lot of sensors, a very good example of analysis that is a lot different, a sense that we will also be having three points. One is basic ground and the openness out, but the guess is different here as the output bin will give a rating, albeit that it's applied to it. Now, if you are giving a final signal to the FCC, it will be giving an output signal that does vary from zero world to all. This ratings signal is called an analog signal that it will be depending on the analog output depending on the temperature of the environment. So this is the analog to digital conversion process. Let's take the same since that thermocouple now, the temperature is right to the analog since up to the analog sensor, and this analog sensor will convert the temperature and the spectra always and it is given to the amplifier since this voltage that it is giving this very low will be available in all, this amplifier will boost that believer to by the microcontroller, then the voltages for the analog to digital converter. So this analog to digital converter will not be an analog signal given to it to be digital format. And this digital signal output from the ABC is given to the microcontroller and this microphone to body for the processing. Most probably, you will be using the ADC model that is available in SATA microcontroller, so these two successes will be mostly inside a single chip and we will not be using any ices for converting the analog. It's sickness. Most commonly used resolution for is, Ben, but that's the reason that this means it will be having values of stupid about this one zero two four. The value will be varying from zero to one zero two three. So using this formula, you can calculate the step size of ABC this week will be looked at about minus one. If you are having the microcontroller that is working on 3.3 World. Then you can buy the pantry, there will be one zero two four minus one. Then this device will be three point two three million. That's it. For each step, this is the oldest variation for anything zero. Two steps will be having a word of zero work and the first will be having a word of three point two. Three million on the second step will be having your day job.

STEP SIZE

$$\text{Step Size} = \frac{V_{cc}}{2^n - 1}$$

Step size = 5 / (1024 − 1)   Step size = 3.3 / (1024 − 1)

Step size = 4.8 mV   Step size = 3.23mV

Resolution = 4.8mV   Resolution = 3.23mV

Six point forty six million and it goes on, and when it reaches one zero two three, it will be having an orbit of 3.3 volt. So if you are working on a pilot microcontroller, then the formula goes like this. Why would there be one zero two four minus one that will give us 4.8 million? So the resolution of this is 4.8 million, which is nothing but in the zero step, we will be having to adopt a zero world. I mean, the first step, we will be having an average of 4.8 million. And when the IDC's readings against it will be having an voltage of 4.8 plus 1.8 9.6 million. And it goes something like this when the LCD is just one zero two three one zero three three steps, then the voltage is 500. An ABC uses successive approximation methods for converting and finding the analogue values. So let's understand all the sectors you approximate in such an approximate city analog signal that it is receiving. So we will not be going in this circle, but we will be just. Getting to know all the sectors you approximate, it is working. So this is a set for successive approximations. So, yeah, testy analog input, and this is difficult. Things are good for analog and this is a company that is the non-voting terminal of the umbrella and this is not the dominant output of these competitors given to the successive approximation register. So dismal output that digital signal of resolution. Then let's take the same in. But the resolution of ATC may vary depending on the microcontroller. Some microcontrollers will be having a ball or aid with NFC, so this will output a better one. But no, we are just assuming that we are using it with NFC, so it will output it in big data. So this back will further build this and not just in big data and analog and it will do this. Do you not think Dominello Company? So the logic is simple, when this is this terminal, this is a higher voltage than this double the output of this competitor, will it be height? And when this terminal is having an Old-Age less than this terminal, then the output of the compressor will be low. So let's assume. This is a bit.

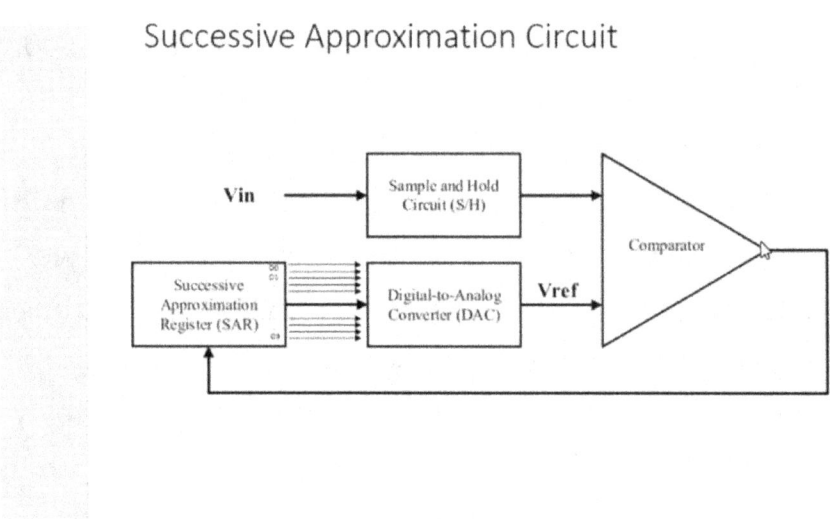

And let's say the value of Onalaska is 250 million to 200. Let's see how this approximates since that finalizes this value and approximates this value. So intent with. Devalue 200 percent at zero zero one one zero zero one zero. So this 200 is given to the company. And initially the speed of this zero, so this 200 is greater than beat up and now be successful approximation to distill output is zero that is mentioned here zero zerozerozero zerozerozero zerozerozero that has been bid value. So when this 200 is greater than zero, the output of the competitor will be one. Right.So this one is a pretty successful approximation to. So this oneness, but they're given to the must be of the output of successive approximations to justify this given here. So this value is nothing but Bible in binary. So now the Fightful value is given to the digital to analog converter and this analog well, if I said to the company as this now, despite what it is greater than the one that so the output of the competitor will be zero. When this is zero zero set to these successive approximations registered and this zero, this will replace the current one where some of the. Successive approximation, but instead, and that one will be shifted to the right by one, but. So the output of the ASEAN will be zero one zerozerozerozerozerozerozerozero. So this value is nothing but 256. But for the company. So no one saw you can see two capacities greater than 200. But the output of the competition will be zero. So again, it is zero for Assaad. Output will be. Replace this one with zero, and it will move the one to the right by one, but so we will get out of zero zero one zero zerozerozerozerozero, which is nothing but one can be a. So this 120 is 120 acres for the comparative non terminal. So you can see the one that is greater than. So the output of the competitors is now the one given to the SCA. Now you can see this one will replace the. Current one percent of the current one percent will be moving to be one, but so the output of the citizens of proximas in the district will be zero zero one one zero zerozerozerozerozero. Which is nothing but 192 against one that is greater than 192 competitors will be born again since it is one successive approximation, but that output will be replacing this one with. This one with one and it will move this one to the right by one bit. So you can see zero zero one oneone zero zero is the output of the successive approximation register, which is nothing but equal before. So now you can see what people are looking for is greater than doing so, the output of the competitor will be zero. So now it doesn't look as if zero zero output will replace this one with zero and it will move this one to the right by one bit. So the output will be zero zero one one zero one zero zero, which is nothing but do not again to not it is greater than 200, so the output of the competitor will be zero. So again, things are to zero. This is what is replaced by zero in the asset output and this one will be moved to the right by one bit. But output will be zero zero one one zero zero one zero one one zero zerozero, which is nothing but wonder. So nobody inverting a non-voting dominance of the competitors equal so it will not output any signal. And thus the statistical approximation settles approximately the analogue signal that it is receding. So this is the method used by most of the ADC models in the microcontroller. I hope you understand how analog signals convert to digital signals and see the microcontroller, you'll see success to approximate.

ADC REGISTER CONFIGURATION IN ARDUINO

let's try to configure our ABC model of over ordinal or fitting analogue signals. Let's get started. So our editing model that is available in over at 7:57 microcontroller ordinarily is soft and translucent, so it will be having values of zero to total. About 10, that is one zero two four. And this tips for configuring this ABC model, this one. So we are just going to implement all the steps and the first step, but we just want to enable the global animal, but we are just going to push to the analog values using the interpreter. So I'm enabling this. But as I said in a previous project, we will be calling this EFCA function or enabling the global and enabling a bit of a microcontroller. 7:57. And the next step, we just want to set the reference voltage to zero, that is we are not going to use the reference voltage from our microcontroller. So I am disabling the reference voltage pin that can be done by going to the register description of the analog to digital conversion. And you can see in this INDYMAC'S register these two bits. Audio Yes. One audio zero defines the reference or. So if I'm clearing these two pins, internal beta will be turned off if I'm giving the value zero one to these two bits. You're mixing with an external capacitor will be selected if I provide the value one zero. These bits will be resolved and if I get the value of one one internal one point one note all day, the difference will be taken up until late. So I'm creating these two bits in the INDYMAC'S register. So using this, I'm selecting No. Internal. Reference, albeit. On the next step, we just want to set it to be a better alignment in a better register.

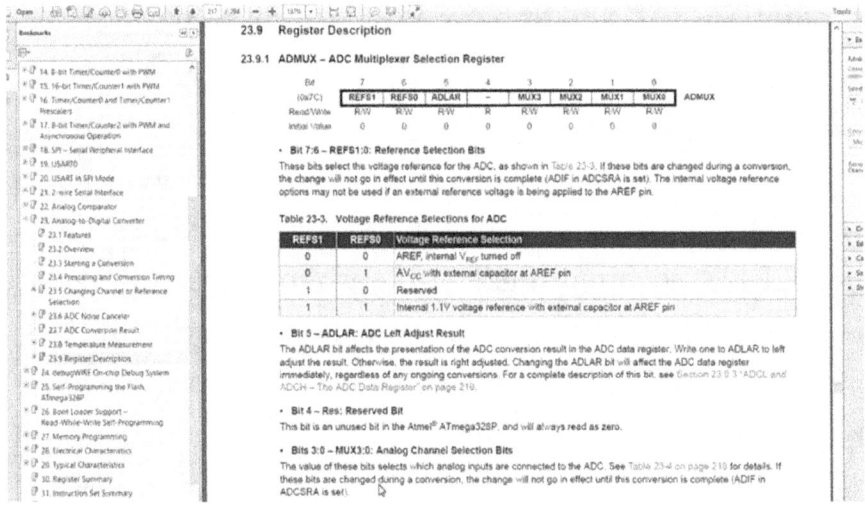

So as I said, we are having a team with ANC, so the value of the ANC will be from zero to one zero two three. But our microcontroller is an eight bit microcontroller. So for storing that pin with value, our microcontroller has to register a bit. That is an ABC hit. And the ABC will. So if they provide the value of zero to maybe elaborate, then the right justification is to select this among the 10 values of the ADC. Yeah, eight boots will be available in the agency, y'all, and the must be toolbox will be available in the next bill. It is the kit. So this will be the data arrangement in these two registers if the Bit British set to zero. And if they give the value of one to any and they are registered, then just if it gives them a select that is the least bit toolbox of economic value will be available in the year. Must be two bits of ADC yield register and you must be eight bits of PIN with ADC. Value will be provided in the ABC hits register. So if you are selecting the left, it has to be given by giving a one to this bet. Then you just want to write off the value by six times before loading this data to any private variable. So I'm selecting the right justification by giving you zero two. Maybe you are with so you can see this in there, but it's also available in the INDYMAC'S register, so I'm clearing that. Right. Just to be selected. Then after that, we just want to enable the ABC and we want to say to the police killer for the ABC. So in this step, we are just going to see them. The ADC yesterday registered just nothing but ADC control and status register eight. So in this register, we just want to enable several bits. If we just want to enable this edition, which is the ADC, enable it, which will enable the ADC model of all the microcontrollers. And then we just want to enable the EAB, i.e. we just think it is enabled. So for enabling the entity, we just want to set this bet. So we are going to use the interface. So I'm enabling this. But also after that, we just want to enable this year that we just do nothing but. Anything auto triggers anybody, so for triggering the ABC can listen automatically, we just want to say this, but so I'm enabling this, but also in this register and using these three bits the ADP. Yes, two two ADP, yes. Zero. We have said please scale what the ABC wasn't.

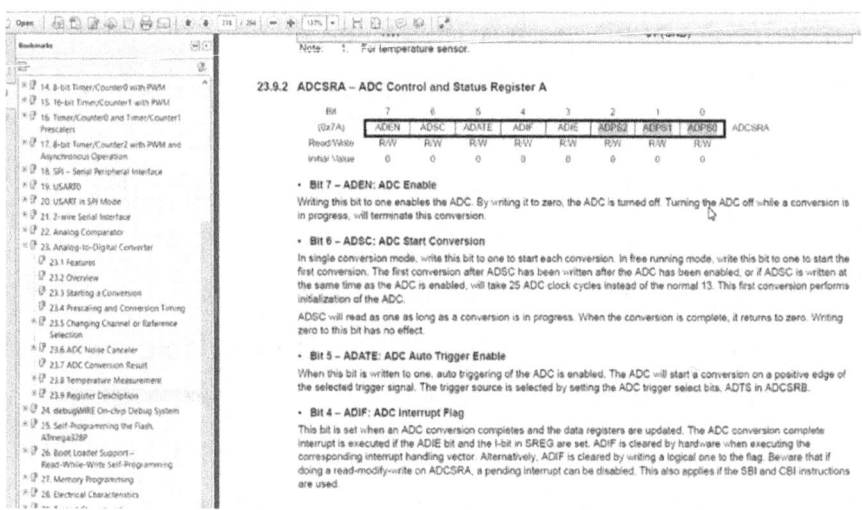

So I want the preschoolers to be 16, so I am setting myself up. Yes, to and I'm clearing the baby just one zero. So the ABC conversation will be of one megahertz, which is nothing but our system clock of 16 Maggart. So 16 by 16 will give me one Maggart I think ABC can clock. So I'm just going to. Said Eddie, Ian Eddie, I usually just two, and I'm just going to clear the creepiest one and maybe zero. And also, I will be sitting in it. AC SRT article to.Idiom.Or one of top 80, 80.Are.Wonders of tough.Yet it. Order one, lots of tough ATP. Yes. And they will clear it. And I went near the ellipse zero on just one. So this will enable the ABC and said today. Please scale up to be 16. So the. Clock of ATC will be equal to 16 megahertz and the system clock will be 16 with just nothing but. One maggot. So one maggot, 60, 80 can move some of our microcontrollers. And the next step was we just wanted to start the conversation. But starting the conversation, we just want to set this, but maybe you see from the agency, it's just it. So this idiocy is nothing but insane. Stockman wasn't, but we're starting the conversation. We just want to set that. But it is the Asari article to one list of top idiots.

So this will start the ABC conversation and the next step. We just forgot one step, that is we just want to. Select the. Channel four wasn't. You can see this is the pinnacle of bigotry to aid in this, you can find there are six ABC journalists analog input, zero two analog input by, you know, what are they not? They are nothing but being seen to be sci fi that is 80 zero to 80. Quite so among this channel, you can choose any of the Channel four converting the analogue signals into digital signals for selecting any of that channel, you are just going to use this much three do not zero bits in the INDYMAC'S register. So this LSP for bits is useful for selecting any of the ABC channels in this table. If you give zero zero zero zero to these four bits, the edited zero will be selected. And if I give zero zero zero one to these four editing one will be selected. Likewise, you can select any channel from anything zero to ABC five. You'll see these four bits. So I'm just going to select the edit as zero by giving a value of zero zero zero zero to these four bits. So I'm going to be 80 months old. And they will. Your value is zero too. All the max bits. And you have selected edits in the channel. By doing this step, you can see it is, you know, it's nothing but peace in zero that this analog input is zero ordinal. Honestly, we just want to implement the HSR concept, so the IFR function for our dyno is, I guess, sort of underscored by ADC. So this is the ISAF function. I didn't say this. I function. You can write your own user defined code. And whenever the ABC conversation is complete in your microcontroller, this ISAF function will be called automatically by the processor. So that's all about the conflagration of AIDS in Module four, the Journal of AIDS in zero with the ADC clock of one megahertz without internal reference all date. And we will see the programming in the upcoming project.

LED DIMMER USING ADC AND PWM IN ARDUINO

We are just going to program over ordinal, we think the analog signals throughout this module using the register level programming. Let's get started. So in the previous project, we just configured our ATC module using several registers. I hope you remember that, and we are just going to use these programming lights before that, let us understand the logic that we are going to implement in our program. So we are just going to connect that variable register to the analog being zero off at Arduino. So we are going to use this variable resistor as the analogue sensor, and I'm connecting a lady to the digital benign of ordinal, which is nothing but the B one output compared to an air of 9-1-1. We are also going to use the P.W. program that we wrote in the BW Am programming project in this tutorial for demonstrating this ABC module, that this will meet on the knob of the motor towards the positive side of the supply. We will get the maximum 10 bit value that is one zero two four. As we know, we have a 10 with ABC in our Arduino. So we will get the maximum value of one zero two four two this analog pin zero. And when they move in off towards the ground side of the variable resistor that is towards the ground, I will receive the value zero. So depending on the knob position, this tip value of the ABC will be varying in the unlock and zero or in our ABC model. So what we are going to do is we know that the pwt that we configured is also often a better solution. So we are just going to take this analog value and we are going to give that value directly to the duty cycle of this BWB.

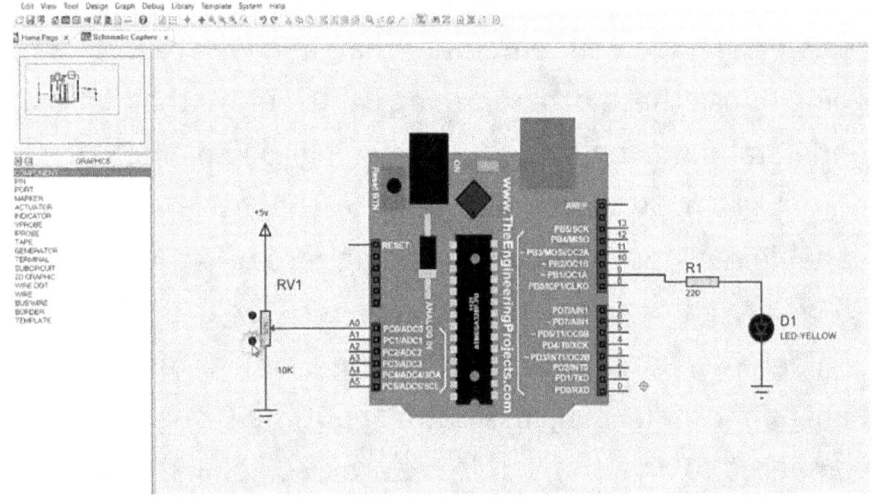

So depending on the position of the variable resistor, the brightness of the LCD will be varying as we are giving the ADC value directly to the duty cycle of the BWB. You can see this and it is connected to the output compatibility of Dimer one. So this is the logic that we are going to implement. This is the same program that we wrote and the problem programming project for wearing the duty cycle of the BWB. And we know that this will see our neighbor register is available for providing the duty cycle of DPW. Its value can be between zero to one zero two three four, wearing the recycled from zero percent to 200 percent it. So now I'm copying all the configuration codes for ABC. And then twisting inside the white setup. Honestly, I'm copping this, I thought, function of ABC. And then posting below the white look. No, what I'm going to do is I'm just going to put this off the Albany value over here. And I will give them we'll see ordinary value to be. Value of the ABC register. And we know that this ADC registered as nothing but the data with ABC. You can either access those individual registers ABC and the ABC it all. You can directly access the ABC register, which is a 16 bit register.

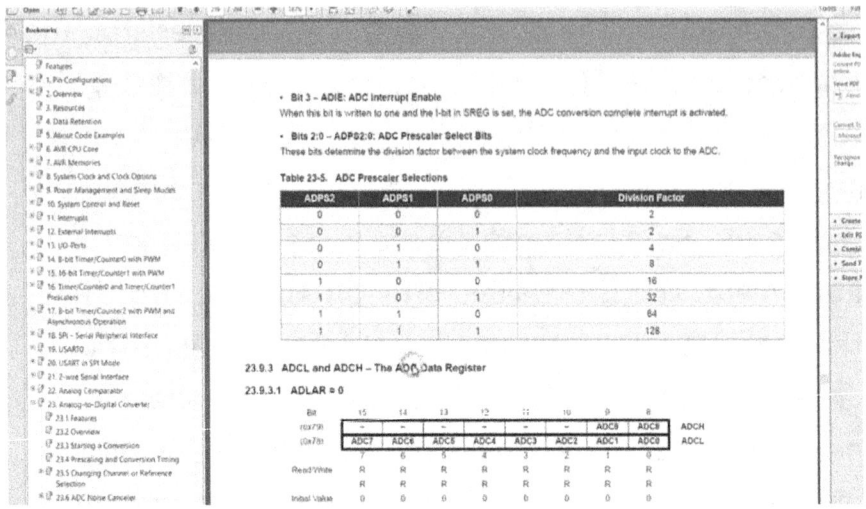

So I'm giving the value of all the Ottawa need to be the ABC, which is the database stuff. It is immoral. So now you can see whenever I really in opposition, I'm variable. It's connected to analog pin zero of ordering. All this ADC data registry value will be varying on this ABC data registry value is assigned to the lossy Albany register, which will be varying the duty cycle of DPW can be generated at time on one channel. So the brightness of the allele that is counter to timer one generally will be varying depending on the position of the variable resistor. So that is all about the programming logic. Let's understand how this program is functioning. So initially, when the program starts, it will execute all the lines over here that is available in the wide setup. After completing that, the program will enter into this wide loop and it will stay here as this is an infinite loop. And whenever any analog to digital conversion is complete, the ABC module will interrupt the processor and the processor process all the process that it was doing here, and it will enter into this ICESat function once the processor enters into this ESR function. It will execute all the lines over here, and after executing the lines available over here, it will go back to this wide loop and it will presumably process it left here. That is nothing, but we have only one line over here. We are sending the ADC data registry value to be we'll see our net duty cycle value. After executing this line. The processor will be coming back to this wide loop and it will be the seemingly process it left there. So this is the robin of ABC in the program. So every time when the ABC can is complete in what ABC model of the microcontroller, this is are function will be called automatically, and the duty cycle of BW will will be varying depending on the value present in the data with the of ABC model.

```
// SELECT THE CHANNEL
ADMUX &= (~(1<<MUX0)) & (~(1<<MUX1)) & (~(1<<MUX2)) & (~(1<<MUX3));   // ADC0 CHANNEL

}

void loop()
{

}

//implement ISR Interrupt handler
ISR(ADC_vect)
{
    OCR1A = ADC; // 0 -1023;
}
```

That's all about the logic now I'm building the code using the tech icon over here. Now you can see the campaign in Texas will now connect to an alternate brought to you what he was. B bought a b c. Once connected, you can upload the program to your order, now, using the icon available over here. Now you can see the program was successfully uploaded to your order, no board, no builders are queued to see the output in the hardware now. This connector alluded to the digital opinion of ordering know through what to do to register on the catalog, and it is connected to the ground. And after that, connect the variable resistor to the analog pin zero of Arduino. One end of the variable resistor is connected to the positive firewall and another enters contact to the ground. So that's all about this attitude now. Power up your order number, using the power adapter or using a

USB port of the PC and after powering up, you can see whenever I really didn't know percent of the variable register, the brightness of a living will be better and correspondingly.

UART SERIAL COMMUNICATION WORKING EXPLAINED

Communication and devices like microcontrollers are of two boats, one a serial communication, an advanced parallel communication. Let's take the decimal number 158 as binary equal in this one zero zero one oneone zero one. Do transmit this eight bit data using parallel communication. We need eight data lines and one gold reference. Let's take microcontrollers one mics to transmit. This number one could be a two microcontroller too. These two microcontrollers are connected with eight data lines, 48 bits of data. As the communication starts, each bit of data will be traveling in separate ways allocated for it. And you can see all the eight bits of data have been transferred to microcontroller two within one block cycle. So panel communication is much faster. If I want to transmit the same data that is using serial communication, we will be having one live one line through which the communication happens. But the bits will be transmitted one after the another in the same blink, and each bit requires one clock cycle and for transmitting eight. But we need eight clock cycles, so the main difference between the balance of communications is that this is faster. This requires less weight. This is mostly useful for smaller distances, and this one is a far larger distance based on the clock. The serial communication is further divided into asynchronous and synchronous in a synchronous serial communication. We don't have a clock then without a clock. All we can know, one bit of data will end. Another bit will start for understanding this. Let's try to understand the simplest form of asynchronous communication, that is, you want a universal asynchronous receiver transmitter in this communication protocol. We will be having two lines. One is a transmitter that is SBX and another one is a receiver that is Orix. Because one microcontroller is connected to the attacks of another microcontroller and vice versa, connection of RDX is also made as we don't have a clock. We need to maintain some common configuration between two devices. That is the transmitter and receiver transmitter and speed data length start and stop. Its transmission speed defines the speed of transmission of data. It is usefully defined in Bahrain.

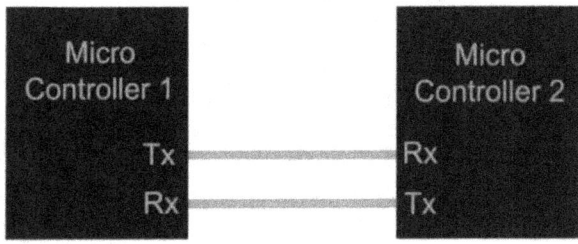

We need some common configuration between transmitter and receiver

Transmission Speed

Commonly used to you, what, Mauritius 9600 bits per second. Then the time taken to transmit one bit of data is given by the inverse of mine six zero. That is one zero four microseconds. So both the devices that are communicating must have the same board. Both the devices that are communicating must be able to transmit data, so either eight bit or 16 bit communication from both the ends must be provided with this start and stop. It's. Initially, you knew what bus height to start with, but as indicated by height, the low pulse on this tablet, as indicated by law, helped us. So the functioning of you, what starts with start? But is the height too low? After that, the receiver starts counting time and suddenly after one, not four microseconds, they get a bit stuck over here. Here, the data will not be sampled as the data will be unstable here, so the data will be fixed at the middle of the database. From here, we know the maximum transmission time of one data, but this was not four microseconds. So the receiver counts down another 52 microseconds from here on sample data over here. One, five eight is represented in binary US one zero zero one oneone zero one on the pulse representation of this data. Is this one? As you can see, this the company gives him starts with start, but that is high to look after one zero four microseconds. The data stops here after all the eight bits of data, the communication stops with the Stop It over here.

REGISTER CONFIGURATION FOR ESTABLISHING UART IN ARDUINO MICROCONTROLLER

We are just going to configure your communication in our ordinal using the level programming. Let's get started. So I have derived some tips for configuring this, your communication. So these are the steps. So the first step, as you can see, we just want to enable the transmission and reception you walk off at three to eight microcontrollers. So coming to our mandatory dataset, which is a microcontroller that is available in no order, no, now you can see that you will start zero tab. So the work communication that we are going to use is nothing but us zero. Coming to the register, Nurse Gibson, you can plainly assert control on capture in a stunning year. We run. It was a sad state to see. So this number this morning represents that this control and status register can be used for any number of us available in the microcontroller that we are using the website zero. So you can get the value of zero this morning. So whatever register we are configuring, we just want to give zero for this corresponding component. So if you are configuring this control register here, you just want to give the names. You'll see ESR zero here. And similarly, you just want to give it. You'll see a certain 0B and you'll see Assad 0C. So the first step is we just want to enable the transmission and reception in US communication. So that can be done by slapping me. Oryx and zero unpicks Ian, zero Brits off, you'll see Assad zero register.

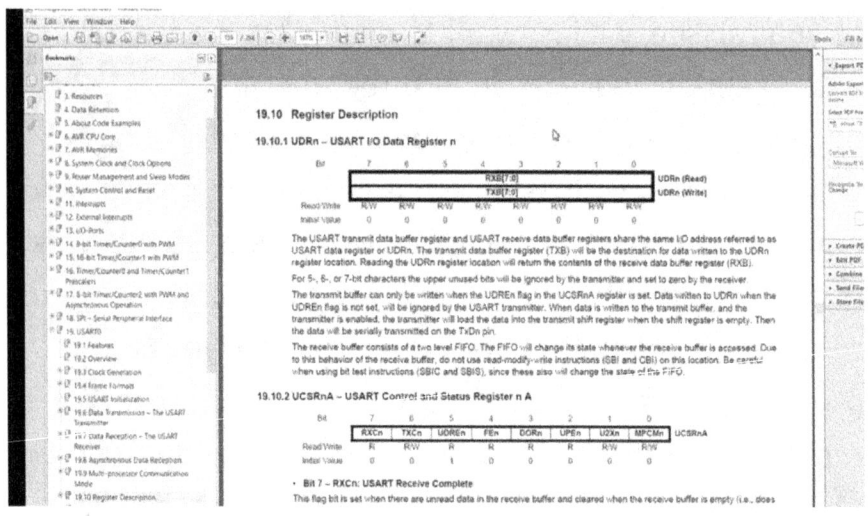

You can see that Oryx Ian Zero is nothing but a receiver. And the speaks, Ian Zero is nothing but a transmitter enabled. So we just want to enable these two bits for enabling the transmission and reception and you what communication? So I'm going to see Assad be registered and then set. Sorry. You'll see Assad 0B register and setting. Are Ian Zero. And six m zero. So this will enable the transmission and disruption in you, what communication? And the next step is we just want to set data science for communication. So that can be done by. So before that, we just want to do one thing. We just want to select the asynchronous work communication that we are going to use. So we are going to use the asynchronous assault. So we just want to like this mode by setting zero to these two bits. They are using Yesil zero zero two Usam, you'll see in zero one. So I'm getting that.

I'm going to see you inside the Little Sea Register. And then clearing the. You see a zero zero. And you will instill zero one. So nobody, I think unless you work, communicate some more to and that but that I'm not going to use the parapet. So I'm disabling disparity by setting zero zero to these two letters U.P zero one one zero zero. So I'm doing it right here. So I have said that the asynchronous mode of your communication and they help disable the beep part before communication. Honestly, I just want to select one stop using this Eusebius zero. So if you give a value of zero to this bit, this will select one stop.

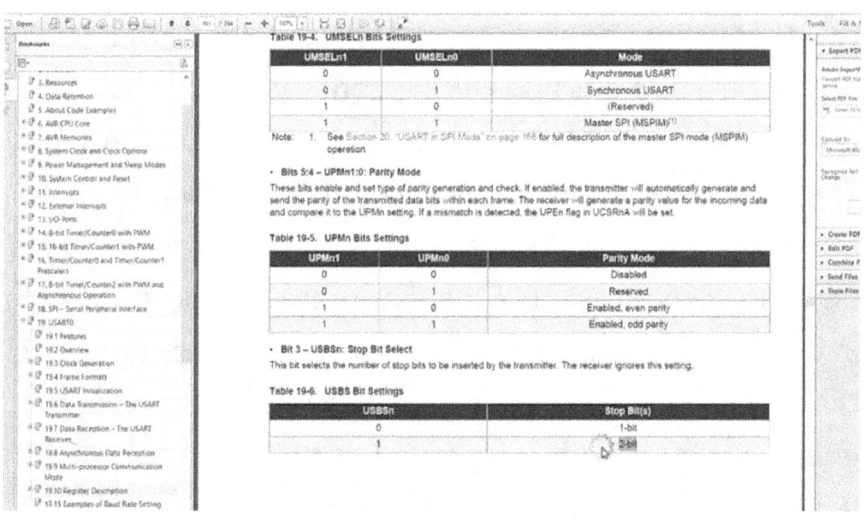

But if you give a value of one to it, it will select those topics. So I just want one stop in my communication. So.

I'm disabling it. So I just want one stop, but in my company, Gibson. So I'm clearing the Eusebius zero, but. So that sort of body control measures to see you controlling status with the sea. Next, please. I just want to. Said to be determined to be a bit. So this government can be said to be using these three bits. You'll see it's easier to do. You'll see us in the zero, but that is one thing. What you'll see is that 022 you'll see us in zero zero bits if they give a value of zero zero zero to these three bits, the data that is being transmitted and received in your company, Gibson will be offline five bits. And if they give the value of zero zero one to these three books, the better it will be six bits. So I won't be able to transmit and receive data, so I will give you the value of zero one one two these three books. That is, I will clearly say that you'll see us zero two bits and will say today you'll see us insert zero one unused. Yes, insert zero zero. And you can see. These two bits, you'll see us either zero one two. You'll see us at zero zero. It's available in the. You'll see Assad 0C register on this, you'll see that there are tools available in the. You'll see Assad 0B logistics. So I just want to clear this button. You see your son, it'll be the duster. So I'm going to see a sad little register. For clearing. You'll see we are up to zero. Yes, it's a little bit. And then I will go to the You'll See US area 0C register. For setting the. You'll see we are at zero zero. And you see us, is that zero one? So now the battalion is selected to be able. Next, two things we just want to say is the speed for transmission, so that can be said using the U2 zero, but that is available in the US, our control and status study. So you can see this is the double the you saw transmission speed, but you find the value one to this, but then high speed motor selector and if I ride zero to this, but then the device of the boat rate will become 16 and it will reduce the border that to communicate some speed, so low speed mode will be selected. So I'm just selecting the high speed mode by setting the value to be one. You do. Next little. So I speak more selectively and the next important thing is that we just want to set the ball rate for communication. We just discussed the working principle of your communication in the previous picture, right? I just explained you clearly about how the data is being transmitted using the you what communication that this medium communication and in that we just discussed about the board. So now we are just going to set the board to be 9600. So 9600 bits split second is the board rate for our communication.

```
// ENABLE THE TRANSMISSION & RECEPTION IN USART b
UCSR0B |= (1<<RXEN0) | (1<<TXEN0);

// SET DATA SIZE FOR COMMUNICATION
UCSR0C &= (~(1<<UMSEL00)) & (~(1<<UMSEL01)) & (~(1<<UPM00)) & (~(1<<UPM01)) & (~(1<<USBS0));

//SET THE DATA LENGTH TO BE 8 BITS
UCSR0B &= (~(1<<UCSZ02));
UCSR0C |= (1<<UCSZ00) | (1<<UCSZ01);  // 8 BITS

// SET THE SPEED OF THE TRANSMISSION
UCSR0A |= (1<<U2X0);  // HIGH SPEED MODE

// SET THE BAUD RATE
```

So that can be settled using the table over here. You can see. In this table. The system clocks 16 maggots. You can see various tables for a variety of system clocks here for maggots. So one point thirty seven three point sixty eight since I'm using an external oscillator of the twin maggots that is available in my adrenal development board. I'm just going to take the value from this table so you can see. I'm just going to select the 9600 board and wait for you to zero ought to be one. So the border is ready. Two, not seven. As per the people. So you can load the board directly to the board register, you are zero, but that is available. So this is the border register, you'll be order zero and you'll be our ZeroHedge. And you can directly accuse them of ordering the oil, so you'll be ordered zero equal to or not. Seven. Or if you want. Giving the value of your two zero to be zero, then you must select the border to be one, not three. That is. If you are creating this, but. Creating this bit. Then you must provide a value of one zero three today, you'll be out of the register for setting the border to be 9600. That's all about the registered configurations. Now we will see two functions. That is used for transmitting and receiving one bit of data using. You workaholic, isn't that the cereal company Gibson? So at this function, it's useful for transmitting one bit of data, and this function is the support receiving one bit of data in your work communication. You can see this function, which is a parameter in the name of see it. So we are waiting for them. You will have all these little flags that are available in your control study. So let's see what that flag is. You will be president. With this nothing, but you will start to register as an MP. This flag indicates if they transmit before it's ready to receive new data. So once the data is in order to transmit the buffer, that data will be transmitted to the user base when the data is completely transmitted from the transmit buffer to the bus. This flag will be raised indicating that the transmit buffer is empty. So we are taking for this flag to be high that you're taking, whether they transmit before us MP and after that, we are loading the data to the Eudaly odds with this data, we drop you. What communication? Once the data is loaded to you'll be audited, all this data will be loaded to the transport buffer of your communication, as you can see.

```
1       // ENABLE THE TRANSMISSION & RECEPTION IN USART b
2       UCSR0B |= (1<<RXEN0) | (1<<TXEN0);
3
4       // SET DATA SIZE FOR COMMUNICATION
5       UCSR0C &= (~(1<<UMSEL00)) & (~(1<<UMSEL01)) & (~(1<<UPM00)) & (~(1<<UPM01)) & (~(1<<USBS0));
6
7       //SET THE DATA LENGTH TO BE 8 BITS
8       UCSR0B &= (~(1<<UCSZ02));
9       UCSR0C |= (1<<UCSZ00) | (1<<UCSZ01);  // 8 BITS
10
11      // SET THE SPEED OF THE TRANSMISSION
12      UCSR0A &= ~(1<<U2X0);  // HIGH SPEED MODE
13
14      // SET THE BAUD RATE
15      UBRR0 = 103;  // 9600
16
17      unsigned char USART_Receive()
18      {
19          while (!(UCSR0A & (1<<RXC0)));
20          return UDR0;
21      }
22
23      void UART_TxChar(char ch)
24      {
25          while (!(UCSR0A & (1<<UDRE0))); /* Wait for empty transmit buffer*/
26          UDR0 = ch;
27      }
28
```

This is the start of the start of your communication, and you can see the transmit buffer and receive appropriate communication will be fighting the same register. So if you right to this register, then the data will be going to the transmit buffer of your communication. And if you read from this register, then the data will be read from the receivable four of the work communication. That is the only difference. So we are waiting for the transport buffer to be empty, and if this jumpy that is indicated by the Eubie added zero, but then we are loading the data to the data register. If you are communicating, that is you are zero. And let's come to the rescue function, so this function receives one bit of data from what was. So we just want to call this one thing using a variable for receiving the data and in this function, we are just checking for the ORIX sees zero bit from the U.S. Condolence Status Register eight. So let's see what is that? So this is the Orexin zero and this is the US receive complete. But. This flag, the said, when there is unreleased data in the received buffer and cleared when they receive offers empty, so when no one complete byte of data is received in the receivable of you communicates in. Unwillingness unread by the process that this flag will be raised. So when we leave the data that is available in the what bus, then this flag will be automatically cleared by the hardware. So we are taking for the received buffer to be full and we are returning the value present and the better stuff you are communicating. So we are taking for the D.C. budget to be full with the data that is unread and input is available. We are returning the value that is present in the data register of what company Kisen. So we will be calling this function often using this format. So the data that is available in the data registry of your company, given that you would be Oslo, will be loaded to the variable called data. And hence, this function is useful for reading one bit of data from you, one bus. And this function is useful for transmitting one complete byte of data to your boss. And that's all about the conflict isn't part of your communication in order? No. These are the functions that we are going to use for transmitting and receiving one complete byte of data in your purse. And let's implement the program in the next project.

HC-05 BLUETOOTH MODULE TESTING

let just the seeds of a Bluetooth module throughout B.C.. Let's get started. Hardware components require USB. What do people convert? Under its seasonal Bluetooth module. Correctly had three 05 Bluetooth modules to you, what people converter, according to the circuit breaker, that this firewall to firewall around the ground and RTX of its face, current topics of people converter and peaks of zero files connected to audits of digital converter. And then connect the usability you walk on water to your PC, USB port. Once after that, right click on this PC and go to properties. And then on device manager. We conduct. And under the Ports tab, you can see that speaking to you is counter to comfort? Please note this No. And you just want this piece of that. This is very low, so sort of software, you can download the software by the link that is provided in the description. Open that. And click on serial radio button and 00:30 Boris to be 9600 if it is not given and no change the call to complete, we just not verified that and then click on Open. You can see the terminal is open now we will. Sender character from a mobile application, so that will be displayed in this permanent. Now in your mobile go to settings. In that got a Bluetooth Anton on Bluetooth, he had my bad adivasis devices identified since I am using it already. No, I'm just going to forget this bad device. I would feel good about this. No, no, I'm starting my Bluetooth. You can see the available devices that it's ideal for, you know, we just want to pad with mostly the password for this will be one two three four zero zero zero zero. Clicking on that? And I'm giving one, two, three, four economies. Yes, it is bad. And now you just want to download this audio Bluetooth app link provided in the downloads section. Open that.

You can see the character traits of a pop up. And go to the buttons and slide a tab. You can see six buttons. The

ABC, BGF and each button will transmit each character. That is a b c d e and f. And when it is Presti. But yeah, you can see, yeah, it's transmitted. And when it pressed the button be. You can see B is transmitted C, B, E and if. Because see, all the data has been transported now for changing the character. You just want to go to the settings icon in the top right corner and slide down to buttons and Slider tab. And click on the comment button configuration. And here you can see all these six buttons that were available there. And if you click on any one of the buttons, it will ask you for the data. If you change the character here, the character that is being transmitted will be changed. Maconochie. So this is how you can change the character that needs to be transmitted. Similarly, you can change the character for each button separately. So this is how it's easier to find Bluetooth models that reveal character from the mobile application. In the next project, we will try to interface to set it off with the microcontroller.

INTERFACING HC-05 BLUETOOTH MODULE WITH ARDUINO

What configuration project we just configured our order, no. What you communicate by setting the bar rate and all the parameters. And in the previous, it's a zero for a testing project. We just worked on it, see zero for using the serial terminal in our PC that is using our Android mobile application. And in this project, we are just going to interface the idea of a Bluetooth module to our Arduino for controlling the onboard, an idea of not using our Android mobile application. Let's get started. So these are the configurations that we did in the youWhat Configuration project. I'm copying all these things and then pasting inside the board set up. And these are the functional definitions that we discussed. I'm copying and pasting and body wipes are the. I hope I hope you remember this thing. So in the previous cathedral protesting project, we just can't forget our Android mobile application in such a way that whenever I press this button, it will transmit correctly and whenever I press this button, this will transmit data correctly. So what we are going to do is we are just going to turn on the LCD that is available and may order not whenever a character is received. And we are just going to turn off the LCD when no character is used to say that is nothing. But whenever I press this button, the LCD will be lit up, and whenever I press this button, the lady will be turned off. So this is the logic that we are going to implement. So this one is the onboard energy that is available in no order, no board. And we know that. This onboard al-Libi is connected to the digital, there'd be no order, no, which is nothing, but maybe five of bigotry to eight.

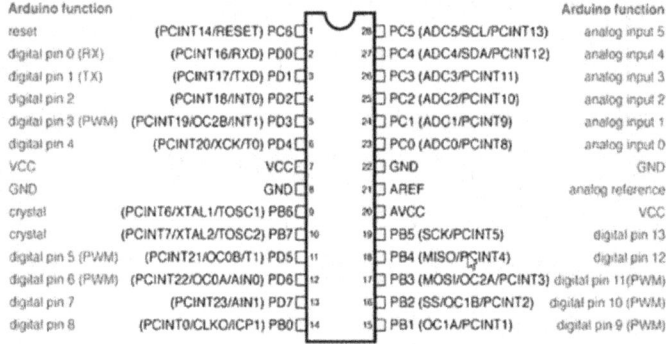

So we just want to configure this business output before using this. So coming into the void setup, I will just configure the business output that can be done by selecting the BBB favorite of B R B registered. So this will configure the baby famous old port to which the onboard

Olivia of Ordinal is connected. And as I said, the logic is simple whenever we receive the correct year, we just want to turn on the allele and whenever we receive the character be, we just want to turn off the entity that is whenever I press this button. The entity must be lifted up, and whenever I press this button, the lady must be turned off. So far this evening, the date that we are just going to use this function, you will receive. So I'm going to use a variable called data for receiving the character. And if the data is small, you. I will turn on the energy counter to be defiant. And. If they. Data is character be. I will turn off the elderly. So you can see the logic is simple and just continuously receiving data from the US suppressing function, using the variable quality data. And if the data received this year, I will turn on the entity if the data received seem B. I will turn off the elderly. I'm just declaring this variable called data. So I have declared to be data ready, but nobody. So that's all about the program. Now I'm building the product using the. I can't here. Now, the campaign is successful . Now the campaign is successful . Now connect to an audience on board through your PC USB port. No character or no development board. If you were busy, you would be given a report. One connector. Click on this Arrow icon for uploading the program to you, what are all? That said, the program has been successful in order for you, what are the known developments? Now.

```
// SET DATA SIZE FOR COMMUNICATION  c
UCSR0C &= (~(1<<UMSEL00)) & (~(1<<UMSEL01)) & (~(1<<UPM00)) & (~(1<<UPM01)) & (~(1<<USBS0));

//SET THE DATA LENGTH TO BE 8 BITS
UCSR0B &= (~(1<<UCSZ02));
UCSR0C |= (1<<UCSZ00) | (1<<UCSZ01);   // 8 BITS

// SET THE SPEED OF THE TRANSMISSION
UCSR0A &= ~(1<<U2X0);   // HIGH SPEED MODE

// SET THE BAUD RATE
UBRR0 = 103;   // 9600

DDRB |= (1<<DDB5);
}
unsigned int data=0;
void loop()
{
    data = USART_Receive();
```

Building sector, we'll see the output in the hardware. That is. Kind of the basics of Bluetooth module to the optics of the development work that is digital pin zero and then connect the firewall of Bluetooth model to defy your world of ordinal and ground of Bluetooth model to the ground of. Ordinal. Then power of the order, no, what you think you will be capable of outgroup power adapter. Now you can see I have the audits of both the defeat of the season to facilitate money under the firewall and of 05 to the firewall and zone audit. No. And they have all of the ordering of what is in the U.S. port of the PC gaming. No maker of this button here in mobile applications. You can see. The almost Lily of ordering a isTypekit up. But don't be.

I2C INTER-INTEGRATED CIRCUITS COMMUNICATION WORKING EXPLAINED

This project next, I don't understand what I do see, but integrated circuits or integrated communication. All this communication protocol works. And what are the parameters used in this protocol? Let's get started. So this is just a serial protocol that is used for establishing communication between the devices that are very close to each other. For example, The words that are available within a single. So I hope you remember this, that people are blocked by the police on the SBA major because this single monster is communicating with these little devices. Yeah, they can see almost we are. You'll see one two three four five six buses, but communicating with three slave devices. So if you are. Using IPC communication, you can see that on school buses, see later on Twitter block to those two buses. All the master and slave connected was the one to do. Once they are built on safety and externally, these two buses are connected to a path of least resistance. And I do see a political sea monster, thanks to the slave device by using it. For example, you can be in the microcontroller. Facebook wants to store the data to the RTC, then will call the address of the IPC, and then it will go to the RTC. If you want to fetch the data from the sensor, then it will call off the sensor, forfeiting the data. So in this way, communication happens.

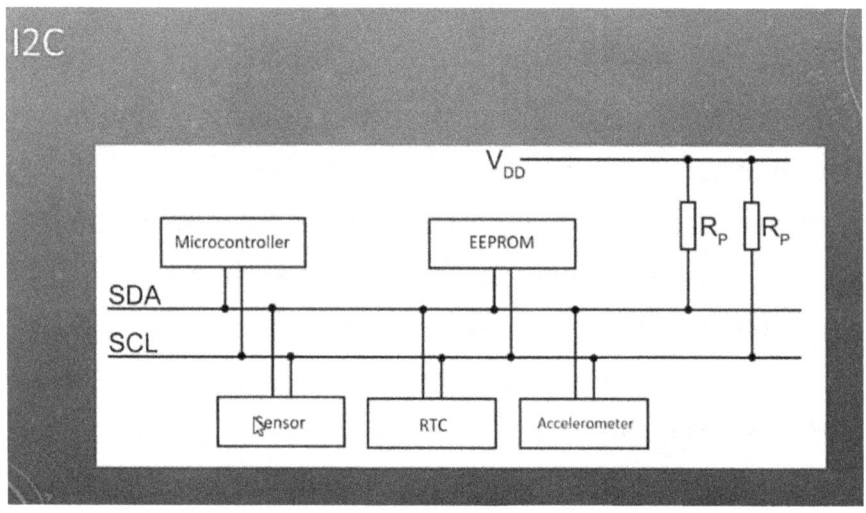

So let's understand the FDA lengths, these two lines are dry drugs connected to the busted supply by opening up resistance. This is to make the lines high. Then the communication is not established. We are doing this because they are configured under open rain automobile collector configuration. As we can see, here, we are connected, this is the year and the ACL is just about 30, possibly at the other end. But understanding what an open drain is. We will see an example. So this is the normal configuration and no microcontroller when we supplied zero over here. This note will provide a one which will activate the MOSFET and it will be documented this month. But so we will get to zero over here when they give up one over here from the external world. This note will provide a zero on the other, which will activate this month, but it will be activated this month. So we will get that coffee supply over here, but this is a normal full configuration of the people. But if you're having an open brain conflict in your. This will be like this, so you can see this enormous brain is free. So that is what it is called open. So when we give it zero, this not will give you one in the output and this will activate this with an. The EPA, what we're going to see Bat Signal 08 when we make this one. They will give it zero and this will be actively deactivated and we will not. I mean, it did over here in this role of the microcontroller. So for this purpose, we are providing this. So now if it provides zero or not it will not activate this and we will get to zero signal over here. And when we have one more overhead, this not will give us zero and this will activate this MOSFET. So we will have to see that one over here. So this is the configuration of the open brain, and that is why we are giving up.

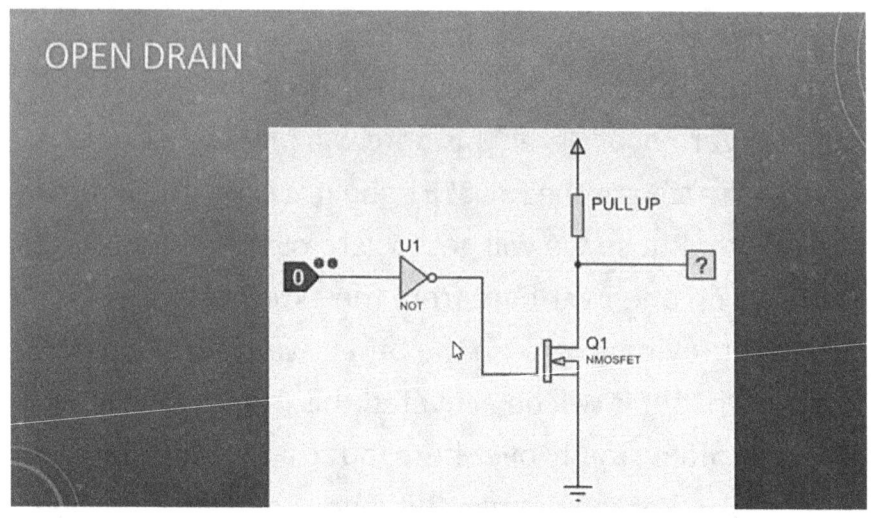

Register for this.ICAC buses. So whenever we configure the microcontroller, the Princess I2C model will be configured at the microphone in I2C mode and will become an open train configuration prince. That is why we are providing for the Prince. The gunman speeds off of Seattle Standard mode. They will be receiving the 100 kilobits from basketball, will be receiving benefits from foster mode plus one megabit from high speed. We will be setting up 3.1 megabits. Most probably will be using front uploads and workloads. Let's understand the I2C protocol, but for a simple example the communication always starts with StockTwits the and following the start with the Masterson's address. So in these eight with seven bits of progress, I'm the eighth leader that if this bit this one statistic listing for better read this book is the most sadistic listing for better. And once these voters, given the master, will vote for an acknowledgment signal from sleep and it will receive the acknowledgement signal from the slate. And after that, once the monster receives the acknowledgement from this slave, it will proceed to transmit the data to this little. So data will be transmitted. Again, it will wait for the acknowledgement from the same, whether the data sent properly or not, once the acknowledgement is again given from the staff for the master, the master can stop the processing and say stop it. So this is a simple protocol example. I see so many cases. So let's understand this. Parameters of Albacete protocol. So let's understand each and every parameter of AIPAC protocol, the first parameters start and stop. Start with this nothing but. I do not practice the year when the Cialis hype. So this is defined as an insult, because nothing but not to transition on is b and see in this time.

START & STOP CONDITION

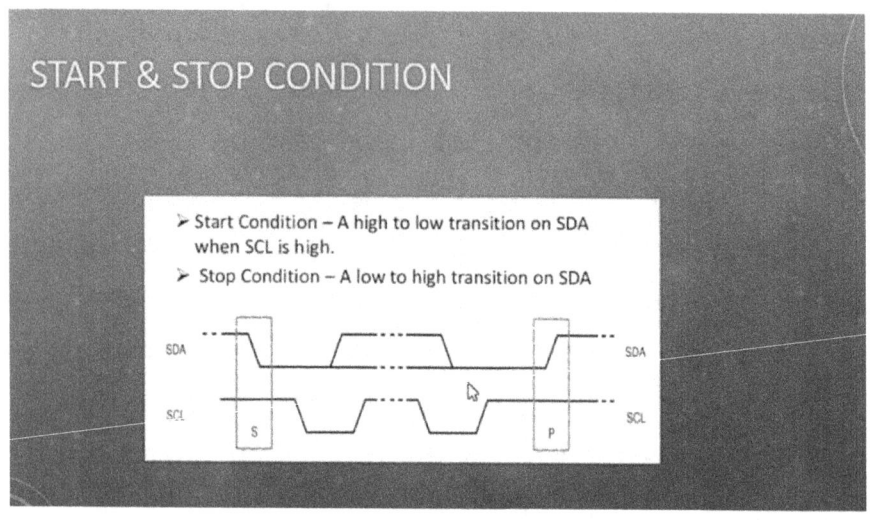

So start and stop because always genetically the master after the start, but the bus will be busy once one leaves. When these properties are given, the bus will be left to play for another monster coming to get. So I took the address face to face as I said it will be of eight bits. That is one bite with seven bits and the eight the bits read. All right, but.And next, but this acknowledgement and not acknowledgement. So once one bit of data is eight bits of data but not one. Mostly the monster will wait for the ninth, the clock cycle. And in this block cycle, we see if you are a line low, then that transition is taken as acknowledgement by the master. I mean, it's not pulling that line low on the 9th the clock was then that is taken us not acknowledgement by the master. But this one's eight bits of data, it's transmitted from the master to slave, the master will release the ESRB line and it will wait for the slaves to follow that law in the nine, the Glock was in fact pulling low. People take acknowledgement by the state. And if it is not pulling, it will take. Please do not modify it. You can see it is pulling low. So if this acknowledgement by this new effort is not pulling low, then it is not acknowledged by the state. So let's see. The data valid in the embassy was so data is stable and the pulse of the clock. And so we can change the data only when the clock is low. As you can see in the papers, the data is stable, so no transition happens here. So when the sale is low, the data gets sent. So let's understand the APC Lite operation. Well, Master, since they started following that, it was in the US along with. Zito. And it is waiting for acknowledgement from this letter, once the acknowledgement is received, it will send the database. One, it is sending the data and it will wait for the acknowledgement from the state. Once the acknowledgement was received. They must have stopped the process. If the monster wants to send two more bites to the slave, the monster will not start the process here.

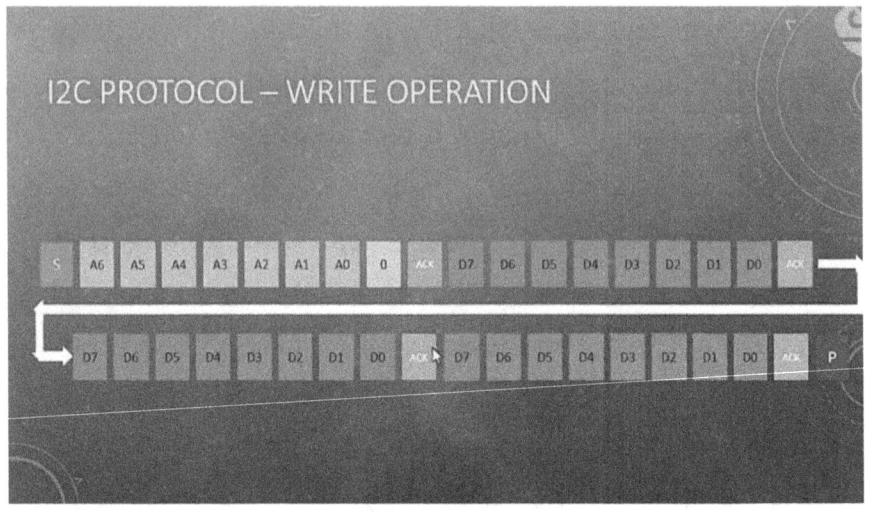

Instead, it will send a database again and wait for acknowledgement again. It was a database getting away with that knowledge and then it would stop the process. See the AIPAC lead operation. The master senses start, but then uses the address along with the big one. Once the acknowledgement is given by this flame, it will be there on the table. And then after reading the master, it will stop the process. Nothing stopping. If it's one to these two more bytes of data, it will not stop here. Instead. It will send an acknowledgement that this is a monster since the acknowledgement meticulously and again, it will be one more bite of data once it gets into our parliament with it. And then again, it will be one more bite of the dot and then after that, it will send a MacBook along with its bid to solve the crisis. So this is the lead operation in ICAC, but that is another one more repeat that started with. So let's understand why we need this for this, we will take an example microcontroller connected to an E. You'll see an I2C bus. If we are having one life, one microcontroller and one is connected to an I2C bus, then that is not a problem. But if you are having two or three microcontrollers connected to the same eBrill, then that is a problem, as you can see. Let's write a letter to the people and then we want to read the letter from the same address. So let's listen to start along with the address right then. Once the acknowledgment of this is from this, it will read the data once again across America, and it will stop this process once it stops. Again, the math doesn't start with I'm following the address with the lead, but again acknowledgement of receipt and the data is from the ground and then not because somebody wants nothing to do with it and it will stop the process here. You must notice one thing that when we were sending this was to stop the FDA, Linus released it. So again, when they start with the still Amos put it below, so we're doing this. I know that dancing for another microcontroller co-led with the same is being late because all our connection in this scene is the ideal place. So instead of stopping the process here, what we want to do is. We will send that we start with the following that we will send the address along with the lead, but. And we will wait for acknowledgement, and after the acknowledgement, we will leave the attack on the same address and we will send the knock from the master and we will stop the process. So this is the main application of this website. And now I hope you understand how I perceive protocol works and what are the parameters you are going to be using the I2C protocol you will see in the next election?

REGISTER CONFIGURATION FOR ESTABLISHING I2C COMMUNICATION IN ARDUINO PART – 1

let's configure our microcontroller's I2C bus for introducing the VESA Test apron to it. Let's get started. So we are just going to see several functions that are useful for communicating with the I2C bus in our 16 microcontroller and all the functions that we are going to see in this project are common for all the devices that are working on the I2C bus. So you can use these functions by interfacing any device that is working on an I2C bus. Let's get started. So the first function I took was the installation and this function is used for setting the frequency for I2C communication as part of the data set off of microcontroller or I2C communication. Maximum speed is 400 kilowatts. So we are just going to set a frequency 200 kilowatt hour that we just want to load the corresponding value to register. But we have a formula that is this one. Using this formula, we know that cell frequencies under kilohertz and the CPU clock frequency is 16, Meghan on the DWP has nothing but praise for the communicator. And I just want to set the political ad to sixty four. So I'm setting these topics and they just want to find the corresponding value of BWB value.

```
 1  void I2C_Init()                                           /* I2C initialize function */
 2  {
 3
 4      TWSR = 0;
 5      TWBR = ((F_CPU/100000)-16)/(2*pow(4,(TWSR&((1<<TWPS0)|(1<<TWPS1)))));  /* Get bit rate register value by formula */
 6  }
 7
 8
 9  uint8_t I2C_Start(char write_address)                     /* I2C start function */
10  {
11
12      TWCR = (1<<TWSTA)|(1<<TWEN)|(1<<TWINT);               /* Enable TWI, generate start condition and clear interrupt flag */
13      while (!(TWCR & (1<<TWINT)));                         /* Wait until TWI finish its current job (start condition) */
14
15      TWDR = write_address;                                 /* If yes then write SLA+W in TWI data register */
16      TWCR = (1<<TWEN)|(1<<TWINT);                          /* Enable TWI and clear interrupt flag */
17      while (!(TWCR & (1<<TWINT)));                         /* Wait until TWI finish its current job (write operation) */
18
19
20  }
21
22  uint8_t I2C_Repeated_Start(char read_address)             /* I2C repeated start function */
23  {
24
25      TWCR = (1<<TWSTA)|(1<<TWEN)|(1<<TWINT);               /* Enable TWI, generate start condition and clear interrupt flag */
26      while (!(TWCR & (1<<TWINT)));                         /* Wait until TWI finish its current job (start condition) */
27
28      TWDR = read_address;                                  /* If yes then write SLA+R in TWI data register */
29      TWCR = (1<<TWEN)|(1<<TWINT);                          /* Enable TWI and clear interrupt flag */
30      while (!(TWCR & (1<<TWINT)));                         /* Wait until TWI finish its current job (write operation) */
31
32  }
33
```

That formula I have written here, you can see this FCP is nothing but 16 markers, and this is the kind of frequency that we want to set. And this color. I'm just setting these to Brittany Dawe AsadoEdition, and for all of this value, I'm presenting it to the DWP. So this one is useful for setting the frequency of what I think I'm going to give some. And the next two factors, I put it starting on this one. It's useful for sending a start to the race along with the flavors of the device. The first line you can see is Gilbertson the IWC, a pretty pest control register that does this register. We are setting the BW GSD that the steam to an interface stock condition, but. Go ahead and start to listen, but we are enabling this and then we are enabling me to enable it. But that is one thought and purpose that enables it. And then we are clearing the way in the best interest by riding one toward. That is done using this line once we have simply started on, once we have initiated the start, but here, once they start executing, this interest flag will be raised. So we are waiting for this flag to be high and want to say we will come out of the sloop after that. We are writing the address today to enter data, register this pwt arrestee to enter basic data instead of so. We are loading the address to the data register and we are enabling the boy and enable and we are clearing me to plug in the control controlled stop the where communication. Once we enable the communication and once the data is fully written, this touring problem will be high and we will come out of this loop and thus this function is used for sending the start along with the flavors of the device. The next leaf, we will see the eye to see the pretty star function. So this one ton of CO_2 for turning a repeater starboard from one microcontroller to electricity ways. So this is the same line that we saw in the previous function.

We are just enabling the start with nimble. And we are clearing the entire flank. After that, we are waiting for the target condition to be executed using this interplay, one sort of executable, we are loading the address to the data register. After that, we are able to be aware and able and we are clearing the board and then we are waiting for the right operation to complete. Using this interface, I wanted to say we will go out of this function. This is similar to the previous function. Right after that, we are waiting to see out of this top condition. So this funding is used for sending a stop condition from our master to the I2C bus board that we just want to enable the DWP deal that is D to interface top condition. And we just want to interface into the plan. And then we just want to enable the enable funding to work on the register, as you can see the system to way interface top condition. We are doing this and we are creating the flag by writing one and we are enabling awareness. And so we have initiated this top condition here. And once this top condition is executed, this VW style will be raised. So we're talking about that in this condition, and once that is raised, we will come out of this function. And that's it. And the next function is I2C to see if this function is used for writing one bit of data from our microcontroller to I2C bus or I2C device. So the first two steps, we just want to load the data to the data register that is pwt on before loading the data to the I2C bus.

```c
void I2C_Stop()                                      /* I2C stop function */
{
    TWCR=(1<<TWSTO)|(1<<TWINT)|(1<<TWEN);            /* Enable TWI, generate stop condition and clear interrupt flag */
    while(TWCR & (1<<TWSTO));                        /* Wait until stop condition execution */
}

uint8_t I2C_Write(char data)                         /* I2C write function */
{
    TWDR=decimal_to_bcd(data);                       /* Copy data in TWI data register */
    TWCR = (1<<TWEN)|(1<<TWINT);                     /* Enable TWI and clear interrupt flag */
    while (!(TWCR & (1<<TWINT)));                    /* Wait until TWI finish its current job (Write operation) */
}

char I2C_Read_Ack()                                  /* I2C read ack function */
{
    TWCR=(1<<TWEN)|(1<<TWINT)|(1<<TWEA);             /* Enable TWI, generation of ack and clear interrupt flag */
    while (!(TWCR & (1<<TWINT)));                    /* Wait until TWI finish its current job (read operation) */
    return TWDR;                                     /* Return received data */
}

char I2C_Read_Nack()                                 /* I2C read nack function */
{
    TWCR=(1<<TWEN)|(1<<TWINT);                       /* Enable TWI and clear interrupt flag */
    while (!(TWCR & (1<<TWINT)));                    /* Wait until TWI finish its current job (read operation) */
    return TWDR;                                     /* Return received data */
}
```

We just want to convert the decimal return to the intermodal. You're seeing this decimal to basically function. We are just going to discuss this function, and we are loading the data to the AWB that is the data register. After that, we are enabling it and it will break and we are getting deep into the flag by writing one to it in the control register that the CWC are. Then once the one bit of data is returned to the I2C bus or I2C device, this flag will be raised. So we are taking for the track to be high for this. They will come out of this function and this function is used for writing one bit of data to the device on the next sponsors. I want to see lead acknowledgement on the I2C Read Act. So this function is useful for reading one bit of data from I2C bus to the microcontroller and then or sending acknowledgement signals or the same data. So in the first step, we are just going to enable the DWP, and that would be the way to enable it. And we're going to clear the way in the flag by writing one to it, and then we are going to enable the BW year from the BW control register. Let's see what else this does, but it's nothing but the goodwill and purpose enable acknowledgement, but so far sending an acknowledgement once the data was received. We just want to enable this one thing. But where communication is enabled, we will wait for the Inter flag to be high once the complete data is sent straight from the I2C bus to the device or our microcontroller. This Inter flag will be raised and we will come out of this look. After that, we can redo the EWTN data, register to wire communication, which will be holding the data read from the I2C bus. I took this little device and once the data is received, the master will be automatically sending in our plan admin signal to display since we have enabled this bit. So this function is used for reading data from the Open. The communication on the next function is I to see. Read next This one is kind of similar to this function, except that we are not enabling this pwt. So the change made for this process, this simple. Instead of sending an acknowledgement, the master will not respond to the data received. So you can see here we are enabling the pwt and we are creating the entire. After that, we are waiting for the clock to be high. And if it is this height, one complete data is received. So we are returning the data to value, which will be holding me. I consider that ensued from the bus. So once the data to receive the master will not respond to the slip, but no response will be taken as yet. Not acknowledgement, but by this limit. So that is why this function is named as I do see Rebennack and this function is named as I2C. Read EC. So these are the functions that we are going to use to see the next picture.

REGISTER CONFIGURATION FOR ESTABLISHING I2C COMMUNICATION IN ARDUINO PART – 2

in this project, let's fight to raise funds for science that we are going to use for interfacing 24 seats, 32 e from a microcontroller. Let's get started. So this 24 seat, 32 will communicate over microcontroller through I2C bus and this from can one, the goodness of it can only transfer and receive data in ex-serviceman or in binary. So in our program, we will be often using the symbol and status for bit manipulations on for printing the data to the LCD, so before transmitting any visible data from other microcontroller programs to Ebro. We just want to convert the decimal data into exact placement that can be done using this decimal to basically function. And this is a written function, and this will return a not exactly small value for the equal decimal data. As far as when we receive data from the form, we will receive only the data in exactly similar format. If I want to print that data to the LCD, I just want to convert that hexadecimal values into ASCII characters for printing that to the LCD so that can be done by using this function X or to ASCII function. So let's understand these two functions in this picture. So firstly, we will take this except to ask you to function.

```
{
    unsigned char bcd;
    bcd= value;
    bcd=bcd&0xf0;
    bcd=bcd>>4;
    bcd=bcd|0x30;
    lcd_data(bcd);
    bcd=value;
    bcd=bcd&0x0f;
    bcd=bcd|0x30;
    lcd_data(bcd);
}

value = 82

bcd = 82

bcd = 82 & 0xf0
bcd = 1000 0010 & 1111 0000
bcd = 1000 0000 = 80

bcd = bcd>>4 = (1000 0000)>>4 = (0000 1000) = 08

bcd = 8
print 8 to lcd

bcd = bcd | (0x30) = 08 | 30 = 0x38

print 8 to lcd


bcd = 82
```

So in the first step, you can see we are receiving a parameter to this function in the variable named value. So let's assume we are giving a value of 82 in hexadecimal to this function. Initially, we are storing that variable value to a variable called BCD. So I am storing 82 busy then in the next step. You can see BCD equal to BCD Ambersons of zero zero. So in this step, we are masking the yeah must be bits of the variable C, as you can see our values eighty two and we are performing under operation of this VCD value with zero except zero. We know that zero zero is one one one one zero zero zero zero. And this 0:52 binary is nothing but one zero zero one zero. So you perform under operation between these two birds, you can see one Amberson one. Well, give me one. And zero Amberson one will give me zero zerozero. And here also, you can see one ambassador of zero will give me zero. So all the LSP bits will be converted into zero. So I will get one one zero zero zero zero zero zero zero as the value of obesity. That is nothing but the value eight zero. So you can see in this. The list is completely mosquito, and we are having one, we must be that is eight. And in the next step, you can see we see the equal to be CD rates of output. So you we perform right if not for in this one zero zero zero zero zero zero zero, this one double zero will go to the must be four bucks. So I will get the value of double zero zero one triple zero as the value of obesity. So this value is nothing but zero zero eight. So no, I got the I must be valued that this ape stored in the variable. So this is also an encouragement. So for converting that into ASCII, I will order this value with zero three zero that is basically equal to BCD, all of the Iraq zero. So when I tried to order this value with zero six three zero, I will get the value of zero three eight, which is nothing but ASCII character. Eight. So now it must be of the variable value is converted into ASCII. So I'm printing the MSP value onto the LCD, so the number eight will be printed to the LCD. And in the next step, you can see again, we are reloading the BCT variable with the variable value that is 82 art. In the next step, we are masking the LSP. You know, this line that is basically equal to basically ambrosino zero x zero? Yeah. So we know that the value was one zero zero zero zero one zero zero f is nothing but double one double one. So you pay platform under present all these two bits, I can get one three zero two as the result of this BCT variable. So zero two will be stored in the BCT variable and for converting this exact volume to ASCII, I will order this with zero x digital. So if I perform this aurora present, I will get the result of zero three two, which is nothing but ASCII character two. So this tool will be printed to the LCD in the next step. So is this function useful for converting excited small values into ASCII, for printing the data to the LCD? And let's see the next function that this decimal typically functions, which is useful for converting the decimal value into ex-serviceman before transferring data to the prom. So in this, we will assume the value added to this variable value was added to only the first step. We are just. But Cindy, it must be. It's incredible, an MBA must be that is a theme starting to be untrue. I am starting to use LSP. And in the next step, you can see this must be offered will give a value of the zeal that it will bring the books available, and let's be of the variable too. You must be. So I will get the result of a zero for this expedition. And after that, I'm adding the LSP value to the MSP lifts of doubtful. So we know that the LSP value was nothing but do so when they add this to the eight zero, I will get this eighty two as the exact value that is getting stored in the variable named Hex. So does this function as useful for returning the ex-servicemen equal in value for decimal values passed to this function? So this is a return to a function of God, so this function will return equal and exactly small values for the decimal values offset to this function. So we will see the complete program for interfacing 24 seat 32 from our microcontroller in that next project.

INTERFACING 24CXX EEPROM WITH ARDUINO USING I2C COMMUNICATION

In the previous two projects, you just configure the I2C communication of the microcontroller at three to eight that is available in our ordinal. And we just wrote some functional definitions for interfacing I2C, but what are they not? Now in this project, they are just going to interface 34C Zettl for that I2C prone to over ordering. Let's get started. So in the previous two projects, we just configured the AI to see. So in the previous eight, to reconfigure this and look just part one, we just configured the items the company gives them. I'm copying all the code and then pasting a body wide set up. And in the previous APEC conference and part two, we just wrote two functions for interfacing impromptu over until they are fixed to ASCII. And they seem to be silly since I have decided not to use the LCD. I'm just going to use the serial monitor that is available in May or not. So for that, I just want to make some changes to this function. They are. Instead of printing that to the city, I will print that data to the CDL monitor. The similar way I will do it here, also another printing the two bits of data. I will give the interview below, but I'm moving to the next line.

```
void hex_to_ascii(unsigned char value)
{
    unsigned char bcd;
    bcd= value;
    bcd=bcd&0xf0;
    bcd=bcd>>4;
    Serial.print(bcd);
    bcd=value;
    bcd=bcd&0x0f;
    Serial.print(bcd);
    Serial('\n');

}

char decimal_to_bcd(unsigned char value)
{
    unsigned char msb,lsb,hex;
    msb=value/10;
    lsb=value%10;
    hex = ((msb<<4)+lsb);
    return hex;
}
```

So the labor and presents I'm copying these two functions also. And it's interesting.About all differences. And coming to our logic, we are going to do this. We are just going to go to the 06. Total orders of the EA from 2014 04, and we are going to write the data zero nine then and then after writing this data, we are just going to wait for all of us again. Enough time delayed. We are just going to read the data that is available in the address 0x to do so that this nine million will be printed to see the Al-Monitor. So this is the programming logic that we are going to implement. And you can see I have already written some code inside the wild setup. These are the programming logic that we are going to implement. Let's understand this logic that initially I'm enabling the global enable bit of our microcontroller at. After that, I'm just enabling this serial monitor of the order and over the border of nine thousand six hundred. Then I'm insulating the I2C company, Gibson. But the frequency of underclothes, as you can see from the data, said Dr. Anthony Fauci 04 from. The maximum clock frequency and recklessness. And after that, they are just going to ride to the prom using this sequence, and we are waiting for half a second. Then we are just going to implement the leap sequence to the prom again.

```
    I2C_Init();

    I2C_Start(0xA0);          /* Start I2C con
    I2C_Write(22);
    I2C_Write(97);
    I2C_Stop();               /* Stop I:

    delay(500);

    I2C_Start(0xA0);          /* Start I2C con
    I2C_Write(22);            /* Write
    I2C_Repeated_Start(0xA1);
    data = I2C_Read_Nack();
    I2C_Stop();               /* Stop I:

    delay(500);

    hex_to_ascii(data);
```

We are just going to wait for all of us again. Then we are going to print the data that we read from the EU Prom to the signal monitor using this X2 as a key function. So let's understand the sequence one by one. First, the thing that we want to see is the race address. So this is the device address of the 2014 04 Ebrill. These three are the bins available in the Ebro. So in May 2014 04 modules that I'm having, these three bins are connected to the ground. So these three values of this lavatories, it's No. Zero, in my case. So this is the slavery's of the Western Divorcee 04. And you can see, first of all, bites are one zero one zero. So the slave addresses one zero one zero. Following that, this slave address, it's depending on the that is it all year one and year two, often people see zero four in my module. I'm having all these bins connected to grown, so I just want to give the value zero to all these bits. If you are buying a module, I will recommend you to check for these things. It's legally available in the module, but they are connected to Boston supply or be grown if they are connected to the Boston supply.

The 24C04A monitors the bus for its corresponding slave address all the time. It generates an acknowledge bit if the slave address was true and it is not in a programming mode.

FIGURE 4-1: SLAVE ADDRESS ALLOCATION

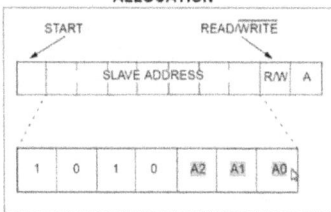

You just want to give one to the respective values of even year to year zero. If they are connected to ground. You just want to go zero to the corresponding bits. Well, in my case, they are connected to the ground, so I am giving a value of zero zerozero. And the last bit of the address is nothing but the leader that we discussed in the IPCC working right. So if it's zero, then the right operation will be performed and if this one lead operation will be put. So for writing to the E from the addresses, zero x gives little. I'm reading from the E from the addresses 0x. Yeah, what? So this is the address for writing to the prom, and this is the address for reading from the Ebro. And let's see the right sequence first. So this is a debate, the right sequence for writing a debate that you just want to follow. So for introducing any acoustic device, you just want to see the data feeds of the device for the sequence that needs to be followed. It is highly recommended to see the data of the device for following a sequence that is provided in the dataset.

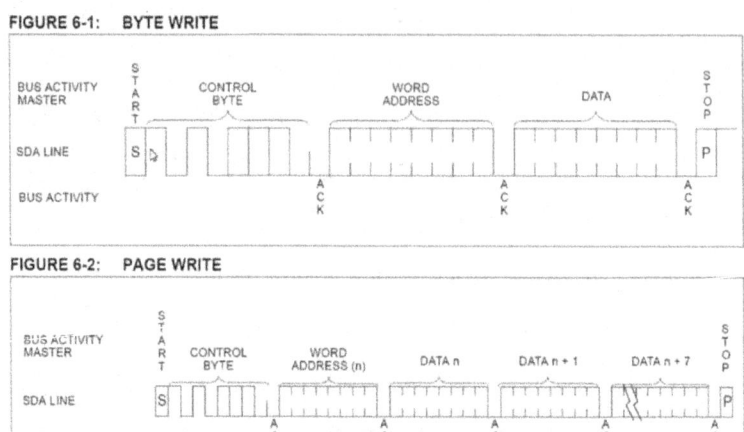

So initially, we just want to start with following the control orders, which is the display of orders, as we know for writing the addresses it looks. Is it all we just want to start the company, get a new thing and start following that. We just want to be zero. It is. So that has done well, but here it does it start this program with zero zero. And after that, we just want to give the address at, but we want to write to the Ebro, as they mentioned. We just want to write to the address 022 of the Ebro. So I am writing the address directly too. And following that, we just want to do the data that needs to be written. So I am going to write this. 99, so after the data, we just want to stop the process using the stop, but. That is done over here. I stopped. So I have clearly explained about the function definitions and the I2C configuration part one project. If you have any queries, you can go back to that project. And after the data was successfully written using the right sequence, I'm just going to wait for half a second, then I will initiate the lead sequence. Let's see the tape sequence. So this is the lead sequence for over 24 scenes, 40 from this sort of start with starting with the following that is controlled by address. So I'm giving this start with zero zero. And after that. Then after that, we just want to give the good address from which we want to read the data. So I just want to read from the same address. Drugs don't do. So I am. Giving the same address directly to. After producing the water, we just want to restart the process. But start with and then we just want you to control the address with read but.

```
    I2C_Start(0xA0);
    I2C_Write(22);
    I2C_Write(99);
    I2C_Stop();                    /* Stop I2 */

    delay(500);

    I2C_Start(0xA0);
    I2C_Write(22);
    I2C_Repeated_Start(0xA1);
    data = I2C_Read_Nack();
    I2C_Stop();                    /* Stop I2 */

    delay(500);

    hex_to_ascii(data);

}
```

So you can see I have restarted the process, but the reader does Xerox, even as we discussed, this is the address for reading from the Ebro and this one of the others for writing to the Ebro one seat controlled by slave orders given with the reader. But we just want to read the data from the vote address. After that, we can stop the process. You can see I'm reading the data using, I believe, the next us as they just want to provide that note acknowledgement, but following the data. After that, we just want to stop the process. So I am reading the data using the I the NEC function, and I'm storing the value to the variable called data after the data is successfully stored and stopping the process using AI to stop. Then I'm waiting for the office again and I am printing the data to the serial monitor of the ordering, all using the X2 ASCII function. Now I'm building the code. Sorry, I just made a mistake. Yet I must give a lot. I'm building again. No, the companies in a successful loan connected to an audience development brought to you what B C was bought through USB cable. Once connected, click on this Arrow button for uploading the program to what order? No.

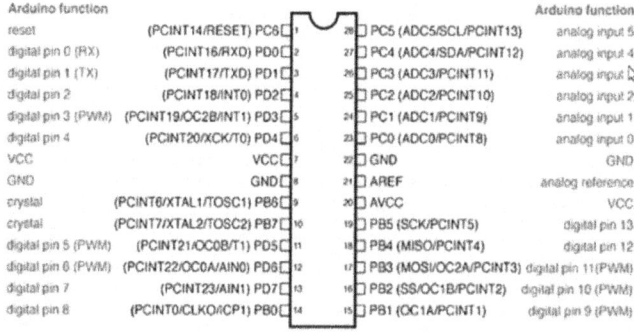

Now, whether the statute will see the output in the hardware, that this word of 2014 04 is going to fire world of order No. And ground of policy zero for the standard two grounds of order. No. You see a lot of 2014 04 as compared to our last 540 no under SBA of politics since 04. E promise to analog pin four of order no on one are distributors bill power of your order. No ball using the USB cable from the BBC and after that. Look at this serial monitor icon to open the serial monitor. You can see 99 sprint around to the seat in the monitor, which is to be done right from 062 to resolve only before C zero four e from. No one trained in the data yet to be ninety seven. I'm closing this window and I'm uprooting the code again with the fetal monitor open. You cannot upload the code to the Alternate Development Board, so you must close the monitor before uploading. Programming is done now. You can see the ninety seven is printed on this serial monitor.

www.ingramcontent.com/pod-product-compliance
Lightning Source LLC
Chambersburg PA
CBHW050050230526
45470CB00004B/1467